Wes Anderson |

Contemporary Film Directors

Edited by Justus Nieland and Jennifer Fay

The Contemporary Film Directors series provides concise, well-written introductions to directors from around the world and from every level of the film industry. Its chief aims are to broaden our awareness of important artists, to give serious critical attention to their work, and to illustrate the variety and vitality of contemporary cinema. Contributors to the series include an array of internationally respected critics and academics. Each volume contains an incisive critical commentary, an informative interview with the director, and a detailed filmography.

A list of books in the series appears at the end of this book.

Wes Anderson |

Donna Kornhaber

UNIVERSITY OF ILLINOIS PRESS
Urbana, Chicago, and Springfield

Frontispiece: Wes Anderson during the filming of *Moonrise Kingdom*. (Focus
Features/Photofest)

"The Reorganization of Life: An Interview with Wes Anderson" is reproduced
from *Cahiers du Cinema*. Published by Cahiers du Cinéma © 2012 Cahiers du
Cinéma SARL.

Library of Congress Cataloging-in-Publication Data
Names: Kornhaber, Donna, 1979- author.
Title: Wes Anderson / by Donna Kornhaber.
Description: Urbana : University of Illinois Press, 2017. | Series: Contemporary
    film directors | Includes bibliographical references and index.
Identifiers: LCCN 2017001733 (print) | LCCN 2017003003 (ebook) | ISBN
    9780252041181 (hardcover : acid-free paper) | ISBN 9780252082726 (pbk. :
    acid-free paper) | ISBN 9780252099755 (e-book)
Subjects: LCSH: Anderson, Wes, 1969—Criticism and interpretation. | Motion
    picture producers and directors—United States.
Classification: LCC PN1998.3.A526 K67 2017 (print) | LCC PN1998.3.A526 (ebook) |
    DDC 791.4302/33092—dc23
LC record available at https://lccn.loc.gov/2017001733

For Cyrus, Sophia, and Gabriel

Contents |

Acknowledgments |

The publication of a book is always a collective effort, and I am grateful to the many individuals who helped make this volume possible. First and foremost, I want to thank Daniel Nasset at the University of Illinois Press for his commitment to this project from start to finish. I also owe a deep debt of gratitude to series editors Justus Nieland and Jennifer Fay, whose interest in this work and whose detailed, thoughtful commentary at every stage of development helped make this book what it is. I also am thankful for the insights and suggestions of J. D. Connor, whose valuable feedback helped the book to take its final shape. Special thanks go to all those involved with the various aspects of editing and producing this volume, including Tad Ringo, Geof Garvey, Kevin Cunningham, Michael Roux, and Roberta Sparenberg.

At *Cahiers du Cinema*, I am grateful to Jerome Cuzol, Sophie Mithouard, and Ouardia Teraha for their willingness to grant me the reproduction rights for the interview included in this volume and for their assistance in making the necessary arrangements for it to be printed here.

At my home institution of the University of Texas at Austin, I am indebted to too many of my colleagues to name them all here. Special thanks go to Elizabeth Cullingford for her always unfailing support and to Douglas Bruster for his friendship and mentorship. For research support, I am grateful to the Department of English and to the College of Liberal Arts and Dean Randy Diehl. It is a special honor for me to make my career at the same institution where Wes Anderson once studied and where he first met his early screenwriting collaborator and sometimes actor Owen Wilson (an English major, I might add). With their precedent in mind, I'd like to thank all the students who first listened to and helped think through many of the ideas presented here; it may be that the next Wes Anderson is among them.

As always, my deepest thanks go to friends and family for their love and support. I want to especially thank Diane and Thomas Dickinson for always being there. To my mother, Donna Fusco: thank you again for everything you've made possible. To my husband, David, and to our beautiful children, Cyrus, Sophia, and Gabriel, I'll offer thanks using the words from Zero's inscription in the book he gives to Agatha in *The Grand Budapest Hotel*: "With respect, adoration, admiration, kisses, gratitude, best wishes, and love from Z to A."

Wes Anderson |

A Collector's Cinema |

In his introduction to the published screenplay for *Rushmore*, Wes Anderson recounts the details of a quixotic mission he undertook around the time of the film's release to arrange a special screening for the retired and reclusive critic Pauline Kael, whose legendary books and *New Yorker* reviews from the 1960s through the 1980s had served as one of Anderson's primary gateways into the history of cinema when he was a student. "I started reading her *New Yorker* reviews in my school library when I was in tenth grade," he recalls, "and her books were always my main guide for finding the right movies to watch and learning about film-makers" (xvi). So it was with no small amount of anticipation that he approached the idea of meeting "probably the most influential movie critic of all time, and . . . definitely my favorite" (xvi). Yet Anderson's effort to present the film to Kael plays out more like a comic episode from one of his own movies than a serious meeting of an esteemed critic and an up-and-coming director. Combining the brazenness and self-aggrandizement of *Rushmore*'s Max Fischer with the decidedly homespun, low-tech scheming of *Bottle Rocket*'s Dignan or *Moonrise Kingdom*'s Sam Shakusky, the young director rejects Kael's polite offer to simply watch a tape of the film and instead arranges a special viewing for the two of them at her local multiplex in rural Massachusetts. It's an elaborate escapade charged to Touchstone Pictures yet pulled off by way of Anderson's own car, which he uses to ferry Kael from her home to the cinema and which he is then forced to illegally double-park in front of the town police station so that he can walk the elderly critic into the theater lobby. After the screening, Anderson and Kael retire to the critic's house, which one can easily imagine as the set-piece for a new Anderson film—a version of the Tenenbaums' overly cluttered and overly cultured New York home set down somewhere in the middle of the woodlands of *Moonrise Kingdom*'s New Penzance Island. "Her house is clapboard and very large, and I saw a deer duck into the trees at the corner of the yard as I came up the driveway," he describes. "The house is full of books," with one room "so crammed with tall stacks of boxes that you had to turn sideways to squeeze around them" (xvi, xvi–xvii). The conversation that plays out between Anderson and Kael in the midst of this clutter has all the hallmarks of one of the filmmaker's tales of tense intergenerational encounters, an attempted meeting of the minds that seeks to bridge an at least partially unbridgeable generation gap. Kael, likely expecting that only a somewhat older filmmaker would be so knowledgeable about and enamored of her writing, seems genuinely flummoxed by the director's unexpected youth: "My god, you're just a kid" are the first words out of her mouth when Anderson appears at her doorstep (xiv). And despite the great lengths to which Anderson has clearly gone to reach her (he even brought a tin of cookies to the screening for them to share), she remains largely unmoved by his efforts—not so disparaging as Royal Tenenbaum in his unsparing assessment of eleven-year-old Margot's birthday-party play about talking animals ("It didn't seem believable to me," he says) but at least as perplexed and unaccommodating as Rosemary Cross in rebuffing Max's own grand gestures or as skeptical and hesitant as the once-renowned but now nearly forgotten Steve Zissou in dealing with the unexpected entreaties of his youthful admirer (and possible son) Ned Plimpton. "I don't know what you've got here, Wes," the famously acerbic Kael tells this unusual young filmmaker who has specially sought her out. "Did the people who gave you the money read the script?" (xvi).

She also points out that *Bottle Rocket*, the director's debut feature that she dimly recalls seeing years before, seemed "thrown together" and adds that "Wes Anderson is a terrible name for a movie director" (xvi, xv). Anderson leaves Kael's residence that evening in a state of mild emotional disarray: "I was a little disappointed by Kael's reaction to the movie," he writes (xvi). For Anderson fans, his unrewarding journey to the hallowed grounds of the critic's secluded home may in some small way recall the much grander expedition of the Whitman brothers in *The Darjeeling Limited*, who travel clear across the world to find their reclusive mother in a convent in the mountains of Rajasthan only to be received in a disarmingly matter-of-fact and resolutely unsentimental manner. "I told you not to come here," she tells her boys, before disappearing on them again the following morning.

Yet there is a bright spot of sorts in Anderson's visit, a moment of true wonder—one that has little to do with Kael herself and everything to do with the objects in her home. At one point during his visit, Anderson recalls, Kael opens the door to a closet in her crowded study and reveals to the young director a kind of cinephile's *wunderkammern*: a chamber filled with stacks of all of Kael's books, those same volumes that once helped introduce Anderson to the wider world of cinema. Kael invites Anderson to take whatever he would like. The significance of the fact that the books arranged before him are all from the original print runs is not lost on the young bibliophile. "They were first editions, and I wanted to take a dozen of them," he recalls (xvii). Yet in the end, Anderson takes only two, and asks Kael to sign one of them. The urge to collect will have to be deferred to another day—or, perhaps more accurately, resituated within his films themselves, where the collector's drive toward completism and the emotional relief such finitude promises is rarely put aside or abandoned so easily as in Anderson's own personal recollection. The fact that Anderson bothers to linger in his description over the books in Kael's closet and his yearning to craft from them a collected set may seem like an idiosyncratic detail within the filmmaker's larger narrative of deflated dreams, yet it is arguably this very detail that helps make Anderson's extended anecdote seem so very much of a piece with his fictions. The impulse toward collecting—toward selecting, regrouping, and arranging for one's personal possession the objects of this world, especially in the face of emotional distress—runs strong in

Anderson's filmmaking, providing a powerful axis of interpretation for approaching his body of films: thematically, formally, and even as a means of understanding their particular status as highly valued cinematic and cultural artifacts. Anderson's is what we might call in the fullest sense of the designation a collector's cinema: a body of films quite literally about collectors and the psycho-emotional dynamics of collecting composed by means of an identifiable collection of (often antiquated) cinematic techniques, all aiming toward the creation of a series of self-consciously collectible (and therefore highly self-referential) filmic objects. As Devin Orgeron observes, much of Anderson's very identity as a filmmaker is bound up with the idea of his own collectability and is "dependent upon the name above the title and upon the reliability of collectors for whom Anderson's films . . . are must haves" (59).

It is in fact one of the most remarkable features of Anderson's filmmaking that every entry in his canon to date prominently identifies one or more central characters as being collectors, focusing significant visual and thematic attention on the nature of their collections and the place that their cherished objects hold within the cinematic worlds the filmmaker has created. Collections large and small mark important plot points in Anderson's films, from the small-time coin collection of the Adams family stolen in the opening moments of *Bottle Rocket*, the director's very first film, to the world-class art collection of the Family Desgoffe-und-Taxis pilfered in *The Grand Budapest Hotel*, his latest feature; they provide the central details of some of his most richly designed set pieces, from the carefully arranged childhood rooms displaying boyhood collections of toy soldiers (*Bottle Rocket*), model airplanes (*Rushmore*), and cars (*The Royal Tenenbaums*) to elaborate adult landmarks festooned with the trophies of world exploration (the Explorer's Club in *The Life Aquatic*) and art history (the Kunstmuseum in *The Grand Budapest Hotel*); they reinforce characters' public personas, as in the anthropologist Etheline Tenenbaum's arrangement of George Caitlin's famous "Indian Gallery" paintings in her office or Eli Cash's public display of Miguel Calderón's hypermasculine painting series "Aggressively Mediocre/Mentally Challenged/Fantasy Island (circle one)" on the walls of his home (fig. 1); and they also reveal their private identities, as in Suzy Bishop's secret collection of stolen library books in *Moonrise Kingdom* or the debonair M. Gustave's only personal possessions in *The Grand Budapest Hotel*, which consist of "a set of ivory-backed hairbrushes and my library of romantic poetry"; they mark inheritances mournfully collected, as in the extensive set of matching Louis Vuitton suitcases carefully inventoried by the Whitman brothers after the premature death of their father, and those joyously bequeathed, as in the set of Encyclopedia Britannica that is Royal Tenenbaum's sole remaining property to pass on to his heirs upon his death; they can represent a narcissistic small-mindedness, as in Zissou's boast that the library of the *Belafonte* contains "a complete first edition set of *The Life Aquatic Companion Series*," his own publication, or a kind of marvelous metaphysical grandeur, as in the central narrative and thematic place that Benjamin Britten's folk opera *Noye's Fludde* plays in *Moonrise Kingdom*, depicting that most legendary and most divine of all collecting efforts, Noah's Ark. Anderson's characters even sometimes worry about being collected themselves, as does Mr. Fox when he jokes about being stuffed and hung over the mantelpiece. It is not surprising that Anderson himself is a collector—the Calderón paintings that decorate Eli's apartment in *The Royal Tenenbaums* belong to him, as does the pricey bric-a-brac that Jack uses to decorate his hotel room in *Hotel Chevalier*. And an interest in the ethos of collecting, in both the most literal sense of the accumulation of objects according to some self-determined structuring principle and in the most metaphorical sense of trying to find a way to bind together disparate items and endow them with special meaning against the encroachments of a disordered world, is one of the most consistent elements across his filmmaking career. Approaching matters of style and film form with a collector's eye for recovering specific techniques like so many souvenirs of cinemas past, and self-consciously viewing his films as objects to be included in some future cinephile's library, Anderson uses the idea of collection both as a subject of exploration and as a tool of organization. Anderson's work, Stefano Baschiera has written, represents "a cinema of objects," one wherein "objects are not a mere element of décor in his films; they are central to the development of the narrative, and, consequently, to the meaning of the film" (118). But this tells only part of the story: It is not just the artful objects of his cinematic worlds that concern Anderson so deeply, but the impulses behind their particular arrangements, even the idea of arrangement itself.

Figure 1. Eli Cash relaxing at home |

In this sense, the focus on collecting in Anderson's œuvre provides a bridge between two separate and largely disjointed camps of criticism and interpretation of his works. On the one hand are those critics, largely in the popular press, who take as definitive to Anderson's identity as a filmmaker only his distinctive visual style, marking him as the "the foremost cinematic stylist working in American film today" (O'Connor); a filmmaker defined by "a high degree of artifice" (Chabon); and the purveyor of an "elaborately pretty candy-box aesthetic" (Jones). For these observers, Anderson is an artist best defined by his "stylistic excess and in-your-face aestheticism," a meticulous and hyperattentive craftsman besotted by the visual potentials of the film frame and interested very little, if at all, in the emotional lives depicted within his rococo art boxes ("Film Review"). "How many other filmmakers . . . could you base your decor, wardrobe and day around?" asks one writer (Bravo). On the other hand are those observers, largely academic readers of Anderson's work, who have focused their attention on the obvious symptoms of loss and displacement that mark the filmmaker's output, what Christian Vittrup calls a pervasive sense of "traumatized melancholy" in his work (5). Hence Orgeron's description that "Anderson's films are all about family structure, its absence, its dissolution, its rebirth" (49). Or Joshua Gooch's reading of Anderson's continual return to the Lacanian loss of the Real via the "structure of blocked desire" (Making a Go" 39), arguing that this "loss becomes the constitutive structure of his characters, his narratives, and his films' constructions" (46). In "Objects/Desire/Oedipus," Gooch explicitly argues that it is necessary "to privilege Anderson's plots over his style," for "once his overarching psychoanalytic focus on Oedipal processes recedes, Anderson's films threaten to disintegrate into little more than the stylistic cues that have defined his cultural uptake" (182). To those who look beyond the careful design of Anderson's frames, the universe depicted inside those brightly colored and well-ordered images can be decidedly dark and disordered—so much so that J. M. Tyree even hazards a visually and temperamentally counterintuitive but thematically resonant comparison between Anderson and filmmaker Todd Solondz, seeing in both directors a highly ambivalent relationship to childhood and an obsession with "home as a place that feels unsafe yet inescapable—to stay is fatal, to return is perilous, to flee for good is ultimately impossible" (26). For every childhood fantasy indulged in Anderson's filmmaking, from bespoke tree houses perched deliriously far above the ground to beautiful pink hotels that look like giant pastries, there is an equally prevalent number of very disturbing adult realities: two divorces, three absentee parents, three struggles with cancer, two deaths from infection, seven tragic deaths by accident (including two depicted on screen), two attempted suicides (including one depicted on screen), one political execution, and six on-screen funerals, all within a body of only eight films—to say nothing of the severed fingers, decapitated heads, murdered pets, and displayed corpses that also mark his world.

For those critics who have looked across from style to content and back again, the effect can be more than a little disorienting. Some observers have accused Anderson of being disconcertingly disengaged in his presentation of acute trauma and loss. His films, Mark Browning writes, lack any "tragic depth of feeling" and present, regardless of the depth of diegetic challenges confronted, only "characters who float in a childish realm, almost in their own amniotic fluid, detached from the real world" (151). Jeffrey Sconce has famously linked Anderson's perceived detachment to the style of "smart film" that he says defines independent cinema and independent-minded Hollywood productions of the 1990s and early aughts, a form of filmmaking that is "particularly attached to the trope of irony" (353) as a means "to laugh at, or express our disengagement from, those around us" (352).[1] Yet this projection of cool irony in the face of diegetic tragedies as profound as those Anderson chooses to engage has struck some observers as a matter of downright cruelty. Anderson, writes Eileen Jones, "candy-coats a world of casual nastiness in bright colors and hummable tunes, and death in his films makes no mark, it just functions as a design element, a dash of dark pigment that sets off the bright colors to better advantage" (Jones). For the viewer who manages to overcome or ignore the emotional distance Anderson's formalism encourages, she argues, the total effect of his films is actually "horrible, like a waking nightmare" (Jones).

Those who have sought to defend the occasionally galling disjunction between the style and substance of Anderson's filmmaking have typically done so by reframing the apparent intent of that style in some way. For Mark Olsen, Anderson's filmmaking lies squarely in the tradition of the New Sincerity first identified in cinema by Jim Collins in the early 1990s. Collins's New Sincerity designation—adopted from one used in the 1980s to describe a number of indie rock bands in Austin, Texas, Anderson's collegiate home—acknowledges the inevitability of irony but modifies it to point to a "move back in time away from the corrupt sophistication of media culture toward a lost authenticity defined simultaneously as a yet-to-be-contaminated folk culture of elemental purity and as the site of successful narcissistic projection" (259). Thus, Olsen argues, "Wes Anderson does not view his characters from some distant Olympus of irony. He stands beside them—or rather, just behind them—cheering them on as they chase their miniaturist renditions of the American Dream" (12). The formalism of Anderson's visual constructions is here a kind of cipher, its cool detachment designed to ultimately fold back in on itself. It is in this vein that Matt Zoller Seitz describes Anderson's filmmaking as "self-critical," asking us to constantly question its drive toward meticulous construction and control and to recognize "how emotionally unhealthy it is" (197). Deborah J. Thomas touches on a similar dynamic in her coinage of the term *melancomic* to describe the total impact of Anderson's films, which she reads as staging "a dialectic between affective dissonance and arousal," perpetually exploring "the relationship between irony and affect and the way the tension between these aesthetic modes destabilizes normative assumptions" (97). In Anne Washburn's assessment of this challenging double vision, the interplay of content and form in Anderson's work presents a kind of "literary double jeopardy," shifting viewers between a position of distance from the events his films depict on account of his ever-meticulous style and a stance of emotional criticism directed toward the very detachment that his style implies. Anderson's project, she writes, is a paradoxical one of "creating an imaginary world to speak about the end of illusion," and it is a project that succeeds only insofar as "he always allows his beautiful worlds to be shattered" (11).

It is in the interpretive context of this double bind between Anderson's agonizing subject matter and highly aestheticized form that it pays for one to remember the degree to which collecting and the impulse to collect is always a response to trauma, always based on a condition of loss. The "figure of the collector," writes Ackbar Abbas, is "the traumatized, privatized, and impotent individual, the etui man of the interior" (226). The very act of collecting, of carefully selecting and arranging and ordering in specific sequence parts and pieces taken from a world that offers no natural order and presents no natural arrangement, is always an attempt to recover a modicum of significance from a universe that, in the absence of natural arrangements, can seem disconcertingly, if not horrifyingly, without apparent meaning. Hence Walter Benjamin's reflections in *The Arcades Project* on "the most deeply hidden motive of the person who collects. . . . Right from the start, the great collector is struck by the confusion, by the scatter, in which the things of the world are found" (211). In this sense, the hyperarticulation of Anderson's *mise-en-scène* and the exactitude of his *découpage*—the degree, that is, to which he enacts the procedures of collecting and arranging in his very approach to filmic storytelling—is not so much a dismissal of the content depicted therein or an act of deliberate distancing from it but a kind of traumatized response to the emotional demands of that material, an acknowledgment of the human pain Anderson chooses to confront as a filmmaker by way of an active attempt to gird against its deepest horrors. The inherent formalism of the collector's instinct, the impulse to detach all items from history and temporality and substitute one's own constructed meanings and connections in their place, should, as Susan Stewart reminds us, never be mistaken for a hollow or detached aestheticism. "Because of the collection's seriality," she observes, "a 'formal' interest always replaces a 'real' interest in collected objects. This replacement holds to the extent that aesthetic value replaces use value. But such an aesthetic value is so clearly tied to the cultural (i.e., deferment, redemption, exchange) that . . . the formalism of the collection is never an 'empty' formalism" (154). It is, in other words, a manner of formalism born from an acute awareness of that disordered and painful reality that the very act of collecting seeks to obviate. It is a negotiation with the very pain it tries to mask. Anderson's characters collect as a means of retreat and escape, which is always also an avenue to regroup and recreate; and Anderson's collector's eye as a filmmaker works in much the same way, from the composition of his frames to the arrangement of extras and special features in his DVDs. There is along the axis of collection a kind of unity and reduplication between content and form within Anderson's filmmaking, one that offers a means of understanding his visual style not from the stance of cold stylistic removal but as a manner of deep thematic engagement in the cinematic worlds he calls into being, one that seeks to offer sympathy for and act in solidarity with the characters who suffer there.

This impulse goes back to the very beginnings of Anderson's career. Some of Anderson's fans have a tendency to view the director's identifiable body of films as beginning essentially with *The Royal Tenenbaums*, his third. The director's earliest feature, *Bottle Rocket*, expanded from a short of the same name, simply "doesn't quite feel like a Wes Anderson movie yet" in Seitz's words (58). And even *Rushmore*, while notably closer in style and character to the director's later works and much beloved by many Anderson fans, does not yet evidence the most characteristic hallmarks of a "typical" Anderson film in its visual composition and choice of subject. As Jonathan Romney wrote upon first encountering Anderson's newly distinctive visual style in *Tenenbaums* when the film was released, "Even to those who relished the otherworldly strangeness of Anderson's last film *Rushmore . . . The Royal Tenenbaums* must come as a surprise, a genuine UFO among American screen comedies" (13). Yet the interest in collecting as a means to accessing and understanding a particular kind of traumatized response to the world is as strongly evident in the narrative and thematics of Anderson's very earliest films as it is in his latest releases, even if the visual analog to such thematic considerations is only still forming in those early works. In fact, *Bottle Rocket* begins in an obsession over collections and the art of distinguishing those that can be disrupted and those that cannot, those that can brook reformation and those that must be kept together. Acting out a practice burglary on his own childhood home in the opening minutes of the film, Anthony provides his scheming and overeager partner Dignan a detailed inventory of those items that they can pilfer and those that must remain untouched. It is telling that the family's prized coin collection, boxed together in a special collector's case, is deemed ripe for liquidation, but more fungible collections found around the house are not. In fact, Anthony stops midburglary—during what is supposed to be a rapidly paced operation—to adjust the arrangement of his childhood collection of toy soldiers, carefully repositioning a figure that has come out of place (fig. 2). Control over the arrangement of our lived world is desperately important to Anderson's characters in whatever small ways it can be achieved. Correspondingly, Anthony is incensed when he learns that Dignan has stolen a pair of earrings against the instructions of his special list, the earrings being a present he gave to his mother that he does not want disturbed—even though mother and child are presumably now estranged. "I know you remember the list 'cause you signed it. You signed the things Dignan's not supposed to touch," Anthony says in the feature version of the film—a specification made even more exact in the short, where he enumerates that "The earrings were number three on the list. Everything in the mahogany box was on the list." In an attempted act of restitution, Anthony secretly meets his younger sister outside her school and gives her the earrings to return to their proper place, requesting that she not ask any further questions about the incident. "I want you to take these earrings and put them in Mom's mahogany box," he says, repeating only a moment later, "Could you just put them in the box please, Grace?" Of course, the sister's greatest question is not about the earrings or their place in their mother's mahogany box but about Anthony and his own displacement from the family home. "When are you coming home?" she asks. "Grace, I can't come home," he replies. "I'm an adult."

Anthony's sentiment might be taken as a kind of motto for the narrative of every one of Anderson's films: "I can't come home. I'm an adult." The painful impossibility of a return to home and childhood as a response to adult trauma is the literal subject of *The Royal Tenenbaums* and *The Darjeeling Limited* and is abstracted into the story of geopolitical trauma and a lost national innocence in *The Grand Budapest Hotel*. Taken in reverse, the attempt to prematurely escape from a painful childhood by racing into a realm of pseudo-adult responsibility and quasi-adult relationships effectively summarizes the storylines of *Rushmore* and *Moonrise*

Figure 2. Anthony's (and Anderson's) first
collection, from the *Bottle Rocket* short

Kingdom. In *The Life Aquatic* and *Fantastic Mr. Fox*, the narrative takes place along a borderland between childhood escape and adult retreat, with the protagonists attempting to negotiate a kind of compromise position between innocence and experience by way of a renewed and expanded concept of the family. In other words, Anderson's films are always about characters who have in some way become separated from one collective group seeking to find or construct their way back into another: The dynamics of collecting and arrangement with which Anderson begins his career and that permeate the whole of his works is always also one and the same as his interest in issues of family and community, the question not of where our objects should be placed but of where we ourselves might best belong. In Brannon Hancock's phrasing, Anderson's filmmaking is centered ultimately on "the characters' recognition that authentic being or personhood is found only in communion, which is to say in radical inter-relationship with others through participation in a particular community." The question of collecting for Anderson is thus a question of collectivity, of the groups—familial, communal, or otherwise—into which we might arrange ourselves, the places where we might possibly find our own matched pair or our own complete set. In this sense, the drive to collect that so permeates Anderson's filmmaking is also at the same time a displacement of the drive *to be collected*, the urge to find a place and a people wherein and with whom one can feel at home: the impulse to find or to construct a family, sometimes at great personal cost. If Anderson's filmmaking visually represents, as Romney suggests, "the foundation of a hypothetical Cinema of Saturation" (15), that is because thematically it is a cinema fundamentally born of a powerful confrontation with emptiness and loss.

Theorizing the Collector

Of course, the interplay of material abundance and emotional vacuity has always been part of the paradoxical figure of the collector, that "traumatized, privatized, and impotent individual" of Abbas's description (226). In this vein, an examination of the critical theory that has developed around the ethos of collecting and the political implications thereof helps to illuminate the psycho-emotional territory in which much of Anderson's filmmaking originates. For collecting is never a neutral act or an idle hobby. As Stewart prominently examined in *On Longing*, collecting is part of a small set of related human activities that attempt to enact a negotiation with emotional trauma via the objects of our material world, using them both as a bulwark against pain and equally as an expression of suffering. The collector, Stewart writes, "seeks a form of self-enclosure," an escape from the past through a system that "replaces history with *classification*, with order beyond the realm of temporality" (151; emphasis in original). Or, in Abbas's formulation, "collecting . . . is at once an attempt to avoid experience and to confront it" (225). In many cases the trauma at the heart of the collector's impulse is quite real and quite specific—think, for instance, of Francis's obsessive collation of his father's extensive suitcase collection and careful inventorying of it in *The Darjeeling Limited*, crying out with great relief "There it is. That's the other one. We found it" upon discovering the last suitcase in the collection only minutes before the funeral. Yet that trauma also may be more diffuse and existential than it is acute and historical. For Benjamin, the struggle in which the collector always engages is "the struggle against dispersion" (*Arcades* 211), the collection being the means by which the world is made "ordered . . . in each of his objects" (*Arcades* 207). The collection is in this sense a mechanism for achieving some small measure of control in a world that one has long recognized as decidedly lacking in purpose. Taking the scattered objects of the world in hand, Benjamin writes, the collector imposes their "integration into a new, expressly devised historical system" (*Arcades* 205), one that intentionally ignores or supersedes existing contexts and instead, as Stewart writes, "removes the object from context and places it within the play of signifiers" (153).

The collector, in other words, does not mean simply to horde or gather, creating an impermeable bulwark of stuff, but to arrange and organize and thereby to reconceive and reconstitute the objects collected, to make of the collection a newly ordered world unto itself. Intuitively, the collector understands one of the primary insights posited by Bill Brown in his development of the critical domain that has come to be known as "thing theory," the idea that there is a "gap between the function of objects and the desires congealed there," one that would be made "clear only when those objects became outmoded"—that is, when they became collectible (13). The objects of our world, Brown argues, are in their everyday function largely invisible to us, their ontology occluded by the purposes they are meant to serve. "We look through objects," he writes, "because there are codes by which our interpretive attention makes them meaningful, because there is a discourse of objectivity that allows us to use them as facts" (4). Only at the edge of usefulness do these objects begin to reveal their alternate and possible underlying identities. In Brown's words, "We begin to confront the thingness of objects when they stop working for us," a moment when we can at last recognize their "latency (the not yet formed or the not yet formable)" and their "excess (what remains physically or metaphysically irreducible to objects)"—or what he calls simply, their "thingness" (4–5). This is the realm that the collector always seeks out, a realm where the object's original purpose and original context have evaporated or been stripped away, a realm of things to be repurposed and recombined. At the heart of every collection lies what Stewart calls "the total aestheticization of use value" (151), or what Benjamin describes as "the liberation of things from the drudgery of being useful" (Arcades 209). Asserting the power of the individual collector to fill in new meanings where the existing arrangements of the world have proved lost or insufficient, the act of collection offers an avenue by which the most emotionally disempowered can in some small way make the world seem comprehensible again. It is in this sense that collecting, as Benjamin in particular understood, is always a creative act. "The most distinguished trait of a collection will always be its transmissibility," Benjamin writes in "Unpacking My Library"—a point that is both literally true in the sense in which a collection may be willed or bequeathed (a legal activity that forms the central plot point of *The Grand Budapest Hotel*, and minor plot points in *The Royal Tenenbaums* and *The Darjeeling Limited*) and figuratively true in the sense in which a collection may act importantly as a form of personal expression, a kind of writing in objects (66). Collecting, Abbas writes, is always "'a way of telling,' a way of transmitting experience through objects rather than verbal language" (232). Hence Benjamin's evocative description of the motivation behind a particular early-nineteenth-century craze for collecting porcelain dinnerware, observing how the era's many collectors "make their feelings known through cups and saucers" (*Arcades* 136).[2] The nature of collecting is such that the collector sees himself or herself as establishing artistic control over the objects of the collection, effecting through selection and arrangement a logic and an expression that is entirely personal. "For the collector," Benjamin writes, "the world is present, and indeed ordered, in each of his objects. Ordered, however, according to a surprising and, for the profane understanding, incomprehensible connection" (Arcades 207). It is primarily in this way that the collection differs substantially from the archive, the library, or the repository, for it makes no attempt at completism according to any logic other than that of its own idiosyncratic making and acknowledges no standard of judgment other than what it imposes on itself.

In fact, Benjamin argues, each collected object alone often has little to do with the purpose of collecting, which aims instead at an act of revivification that becomes possible only through the pairing and arrangement of those objects. "It is the deepest enchantment of the collector," Benjamin writes, "to enclose the particular item within a magic circle" (*Arcades* 205) that comprises all the other components of the collection; in his or her own mind, the collector "brings together what belongs together" (211) regardless of how the world or history may have once separated them. It is in this particular way that the collector is most like an author, writing out a point of view in objects rather than in words. The process of collection, Stewart writes, always entails "the replacement of the narrative of production by the narrative of the collection, the replacement of the narrative of history with the narrative of the individual subject" (156). By the same logic, the collector is always also aligned with the creative activity of the child, collecting being one of the great pleasures and pastimes of many a childhood—part of what Benjamin calls the "process of renewal" by which children enchant the everyday ("Unpacking" 61). Both collector and child seek to revivify the objects of a world that can otherwise seem decidedly lifeless and unmagical, to impose through the special logic of collection a level of significance that exceeds the actual use-value of the items collected, forming "in every single one of his possessions" what Benjamin calls "a whole magic encyclopedia, a world order" (*Arcades* 207). To the true collector, it is the value that an object holds *as part of the collection* that is its greatest appeal, for through the process of collection some small part of a world that can otherwise seem quite dead is made alive again—and through that revivification the collector's own self is brought alive. The objects that a collector displays, Benjamin writes, are "the phantasmagorias of the interior," an external expression of interior life and a kind of physical confirmation of one's own existence (*Arcades* 14). For the collector, he says, it is not that the objects collected "come alive in him; it is he who lives in them" ("Unpacking" 67). The collection is a means by which to stake a claim within a world where one could easily be forgotten, to demand recognition of one's interiority via a special arrangement of the material world that is wholly personal and purposefully idiosyncratic. In this sense, a collection always demands a viewership, even if it consists only of the collector. The very fact of a collection's existence and arrangement, Stewart writes, asks us "to create a fiction of the individual life, a time of the individual subject both transcendent to and parallel to historical time" and thus "depends upon the creation of an individual perceiving and apprehending the collection" (154). The collection calls for its collector to be recognized. *Someone put all this together*, it says. *Someone made this.* The collection is an aching call for acknowledgment, a pained expression of the self.

And in this sense, it also becomes a kind of politically utopian experiment. The act of collection insists that the purposes given by this world are not dispositive and can be rewritten; neither are the arrangements into which things are initially sorted the ones that must remain. The collector dares to recast the supposed givens of this world according to a logic of his or her own original devising, taking as raw material what was supposed to be finished product. As Jonathan Flatley argues, he or she typically does so along the axis of a particularly radical premise: similarity, which Flatley reads as an organizing concept that actively undermines "any number of institutions and discourses that push us to think and feel in terms of either identity or difference" (77). Similarity, or likeness, rejects identity as being the only admissible logic for grouping and dismisses difference as being a sufficient reason for separation. It imposes its own logic of affinity without demanding total coherence or conformity. Similarity is inherently nontotalizing and always partial, implicitly acknowledging dissimilarity in every instance even as it rejects dissimilarity's own totalizing logic. "To be similar to something is precisely to not be the same as it," Flatley writes. "Neither incommensurate nor identical—related, but distinct—similarity is a third term aside the same–different binary" (73). In similarity, Flatley argues, begins collectivity, the idea of a coming together across difference—what he calls, in a remarkable turn of phrase, "we-centricity." The collection is in this reading a utopian space that is always acutely aware of history and temporality but refuses to be governed by them, one that is always cognizant of difference but refuses to defer to it. Collection, Flatley writes, always entails "the translation of an object into the realm of resemblances" such that "we might say that collecting is a practice for creating a constantly changing space of commonality shared by all the objects in the collection" (82). The collection is a place of coming-together, one that imagines the possibility of escape or exemption from the kind of separation and autonomy that mark the hyper-individuated world lying beyond the collection's constructed boundaries. The collection is a place of belonging.

Or, to put it another way, the collection is a world: a newly arranged version of our material reality, remade and renewed according to a radical new logic. "Aesthetic worlds, no matter how they form themselves," writes Eric Hayot in *On Literary Worlds*, "are among other things always a relation to and theory of the lived world" (43); it is in this sense that Pheng Cheah refers to aesthetic creation as an inherently liberating process, "an inexhaustible resource for contesting the world given to us" (35) and showing instead "another world, a force that is immanent to the existing world" (37–38). For the collector, that immanent world is of a very particular sort: the collection calls together the outmoded, the discarded, the mispurposed, and the estranged into an assemblage of new belonging, a refuge from the encroachments of obsolescence. As Sophie Thomas writes, "Objects tend, by definition, to find their way into a collection . . . when their world is disappearing or has been destroyed" (172). If this sense of searching for a new home when one no longer has one to which to return describes the condition of a great many of Anderson's central figures—arguably all of them, either literally or metaphorically—then that is because his aesthetic vision is essentially tied to and filtered through the art of the collection. For it is the collection which attempts to offer a newly remade world to those who feel deeply that they have lost one.

Collecting with Style

Anderson's Worlds

It is with this theoretical background in mind that we can begin to approach the visual and stylistic hallmarks of Anderson's filmmaking, at the forefront of which stands the director's famous attention to the *mise-en-scène*. Few contemporary directors—and arguably few directors of any era—are so associated in the popular imagination with their visual construction inside the frame as Anderson. Examine any popular parody of Anderson's filmmaking (which have arguably become a kind of Internet subgenre unto themselves) and you are sure to find some kind of indicator of an exacting and eccentric attention to the details of set decoration, costuming, and props—the visual elements that make a "movie by Wes Anderson . . . definitely look like a movie by Wes Anderson," in one reviewer's phrase (Haglund).[3] Anderson's visual worlds are frequently cited for their meticulous attention to hand-crafted detail—exemplified by the seventeen different drawings of Margot Tenenbaum executed by Anderson's brother Eric and hung on the walls of the Tenenbaum house or the five hand-sewn cross-stitch images of the major settings of the *Moonrise Kingdom* universe, each one hung somewhere inside the

Bishops' home. And they are equally known for the abundance of material always on display, from the teeming streets of Jodhpur, Rajasthan, in *The Darjeeling Limited* to the cramped on-board editing suite on Zissou's *Belafonte* containing nearly a dozen analog devices in a space no larger than a closet (fig. 3). In sheer detail and density, Anderson's frame is often described as having a diorama or museum-gallery aspect, having even been compared in one less-than-charitable formulation with "an antique store display window" (Gorfinkel 163).[4] In a different temporal vein, some commentators have instead likened Anderson's visual realms to those of a science fiction or fantasy filmmaker—sometimes noting Anderson's boyhood love of the *Star Wars* universe—in claiming that both seek to build a coherent and self-consistent visual system from the ground up.[5]

Yet to focus only on the obvious density of Anderson's *mise-en-scène* and the elements of accumulation and static display that it evokes—or conversely to liken his visual schema to the whole-cloth pictorial invention of the science fiction and fantasy genres—is to overlook a vital aspect of the director's visual aesthetic, which is fundamentally the aesthetic of the collector. Anderson's visual worlds are not so much built as brought together, carefully selected and composited from the material objects of our lived world in a way that both relies on our knowledge of the individual histories and temporalities of those objects and asks us to entirely discount those associations in favor of Anderson's own new

Figure 3. Cramped quarters in the *Belafonte*'s editing suite

recombinations. Anderson's screen tableaux are found-object works, not unlike the tightly packed and painstakingly arranged shadow boxes of artist Joseph Cornell, to which they are often compared. As Michael Chabon reminds us in his essay on the connections between Anderson and Cornell, "the box is the only part of a Cornell work literally 'made' by the artist." Everything else was discovered and deliberately repurposed. Anderson's *mise-en-scène* is not so much a catalog of abundant curiosities or a vision of some hipster science-fiction universe apart as it is a version of our own mundane world as selected, rearranged, and revivified by an artist or a child.

It is, in other words, a collected world, one that builds its meaning in the surprising juxtapositions that it offers more than in the specific ingenuity of any of the objects themselves—in the "magic circle" of the total collection, per Benjamin's description (157). Here it is useful to refer to an actual manual of high-end collecting and home decoration, Grace Vallois's *First Steps in Collecting: Furniture, Glass, China*, which is cited at length by Stewart: "It is not necessary to have everything of the same period, that, to my mind, is dull and uninteresting. . . . I like to see Jacobean chairs living amicably with Sheraton cabinets, and old four posters sharing floor space with 17th century Bridal chests and 18th century Hepplewhite chairs. That is as it should be" (Stewart 157; Vallois 3–4). Vallois might as well be describing the principles of set decoration in a Wes Anderson film: take a little Jacobean and a dash of Sheraton with a sprinkle of Hepplewhite and you have a visual concoction cognizant of all the history embedded within it but beholden to none of it. It is this collector's audacity that leads to a visual world like that of *The Royal Tenenbaums*, which takes place inside a kind of transtemporal rearrangement of the idea of New York. How else to describe a streetscape as casually eclectic as a child's car collection, where a gypsy cab fleet composed entirely of 1987 Chevrolet Caprices and a bus line running only 1977 GM-model buses can share the streets with the 2001 model year BMW used by Chas Tenenbaum or the 1964 Austin-Healy 3000 driven by Eli Cash. Or a shot/reverse shot sequence in which Margot Tenenbaum, looking like Edie Sedgwick in a 1960s-era Fendi mink coat and flanked by those late 1970s-era Green Line buses (fig. 4), can trade frames with her brother Richie dressed prominently in a Björn Borg–style Fila headband and set against a parade of cruise ship attendants dressed all in white and moving in unison like a lost chorus line from a Busby Berkeley musical (fig. 5). Each visual element carries a weighted set of historical and cultural contexts, and yet each spectrum of references is neutralized by the fact of their appearance together—by the creation of a world that exists, like all collections, outside time and outside history, that is only the expression of the collector's utopian construct. As Stewart writes, "The collection does not displace attention to the past; rather, the past is at the service of the collection. . . . All time is made simultaneous or synchronous within the collection's world" (151).

The fundamental ahistoricism of the collection helps explain the logic of juxtaposition that extends, both visually and otherwise, across

Figure 4. Shot: Margot at the bus stop   I

Figure 5. Reverse shot: Richie at the dock   I

all Anderson's films, from the subtlety of Dignan's 1950s-era buzz cut and 1970s-era jumpsuit in the mid-1990s world of *Bottle Rocket* to the brazenness of *The Life Aquatic*'s total disregard for extant geography, allowing its characters to sail in a matter of days from a concocted Mediterranean island to a concocted Southeast Asian island without such inconveniences as traveling through the Suez Canal or rounding the Horn of Africa, as though the collector's impulse to combine and to compress—as in Vallois's dictum to place the Jacobean chairs next to the Sheraton cabinets—could be actually enacted on the physical world itself. Or that it could be enacted on the timelines of history for that matter: as in the social world of *Moonrise Kingdom*, which announces itself as being set in 1965 but, as several commentators have observed, seems to already be in preternatural possession of numerous middle-aged Baby Boomers, characters who "act more like drifting and self-centered refugees from the 1960s than like the generation who lived through the Great Depression"; or as in the geopolitical world of *The Grand Budapest Hotel*, wherein the nationalist adventurism of World War I and the dark ideological tectonics of World War II are placed directly alongside one another in what amounts to a single European conflict, set in a year, 1932, that actually lies outside both wars (Tyree 27). As Anderson admitted in thinking through the historical logic of the film, "It isn't a real 1932. . . . We're kind of combining the First World War with the Second World War, and making it all into three periods. . . . It's kind of a riff on something" (Seitz 34). Again the collector's logic of historical transference becomes the defining logic of Anderson's filmic world.

For Anderson's detractors, the obvious eccentricity of his visual realm and the way that it seeps even into an eccentric logic of geographic space and historical time presents a kind of unredeemable heterogeneity, what Michael Hirschorn calls the director's penchant for "self-indulgent eclecticism" and "off-kilter gestures" that leaves his audiences "drowning in quirk" (144, 142). If the typical approach to cinematic production design is to build what Daniel Frampton calls "a world that is subtly, almost invisibly organized" (2), then Anderson is clearly engaged in a project of a very different sort. It is not that his worlds are uniquely fabulist so much as they are uniquely open to exposing the eccentricity of their organizing logic. In both proximate and distant movie realms, cinematic production design typically perpetuates a sense of internal consistency and carefully omits what C. S. Tashiro calls "contradictions between the objects," internal visual conflicts that might "begin to raise gratuitous questions" (50). But Anderson's collected universe actively cultivates such contradictions, existing perpetually in limbo between positions of nearness to and distance from our lived world and its extant histories. Unmoored from actual history, culture, or geography, yet continually evocative of them just the same, Anderson's films can only be said to take place within what numerous writers have come to call "Wesworld," a realm where every diegetic element points back to the hand that placed it there.[6] It is in this sense that a writer for *Rolling Stone* reviewing Anderson's œuvre could claim that "when the filmmaker cuts to one of his frequent insert shots—showing us the record player, book, stamp or other vintage and/or handcrafted object they're looking at—the objects not only help build the world, but speak volumes about the . . . gentleman behind it" (Rocchi). Like the nineteenth-century collectors of Benjamin's description, Anderson is among those artists who "make their feelings known through cups and saucers" (*Arcades* 206).

For some, this brand of deeply personalized and unabashedly eccentric world building represents nothing more than a grand extension of the narcissistic logic of hipster subculture, wherein any trappings of historical periodicity are ripe for wholesale reappropriation according to a logic of flagrant self-expression. Hence Christian Lorentzen's despairing description of Anderson as "the hipster messiah. He took the ethos of the subculture and made it the governing principle in his films' every detail—their sets, costumes, characters, and neato conceits (one might even say, their metaphysics)," or Kyle Smith's dismissal of Anderson as an artist who "can't see the forest for the twee." Or else his worlds are simply a manifestation of a kind of stunted adolescence writ large, evidencing at once a precocious awareness of the larger world and a profound naivety about its actual contexts and histories, a kid-in-the-candy-store approach to world building wherein the director feels free to grab a little of whatever looks enticing without thinking through the larger ramifications of such consumption. In this view it is the Anderson characters who retreat from the actual world into their meticulously designed childhood tents—Richie's camping tent pitched in the middle of the Tenenbaum's living room and festooned with the tokens of boyhood or Sam and Suzy's similarly designed tent on the beach in *Moonrise Kingdom*—who best embody the director's own sequestered visual structures. Wes Anderson, writes Luke Buckmaster in this vein, is "a talented filmmaker (particularly aesthetically) whose stories find themselves ensconced in childish vacuousness," evidence of his basic "immaturity as a storyteller" and "his affection for flights of fancy."

At issue in both views on the shortcomings or supposed small-mindedness of Anderson's constructed worlds is again the logic of the collector, which lies close to the heart of both the hipster and the childhood negotiations with the world but is by no means unique to either of them. Anderson's approach to visuality cannot finally be reduced to any single subculture or any one broad psycho-emotional category because it is so uniquely his own, not by virtue of any kind of special auteurist originality but simply because the guiding logic of all collecting is fundamentally a logic of idiosyncrasy—as exemplified in Stewart's description of "the replacement of the narrative of history with the narrative of the individual subject" (156). Anderson is not unaware of the degree to which his visual logic of decontextualization and recombination offers both significant freedom and significant stricture, at once opening the whole world to be picked apart and spliced together and at the same time keeping the historical and temporal realities of that world at a safe remove, disallowing such realities entry into the collector's carefully controlled special universe. Anderson has said of his own films that they take place in a realm that is "five degrees removed from reality" (Lamont 12); they don't wholly depart from our world so much as they try to keep it in abeyance a safe distance away. Which is to say that Anderson's immediately identifiable *mise-en-scène* also is immediately recognizable as a form of personal expression and as a symptom of traumatized retreat. As Tashiro observes, visual design is always implicitly a form of critique and an attempt at fashioning an imagined escape, "another way of saying that the real world is *lacking*, is not good enough to provide an idealized, designed image" (v; emphasis in original).

Taking this idea to its extreme, Anderson even goes so far in some cases as to compose his frame such that the logic of his rearrangement of the material world flagrantly supersedes narrative or diegetic sense, openly acknowledging the artificiality of his filmic worlds by virtue of their overly perfect organization. Hence the numerous instances in Anderson's films of a character's costuming clearly and self-consciously matching the set decoration such that the shot takes on the look of an eccentric fashion shoot—as when Royal Tenenbaum's pinstriped double-breasted suits mirror the lush lining of the Lindbergh Palace Hotel's elevator or Mr. Bishop's patterned pants pick up the décor of his New England sitting room or the hue of the gray in the Zubrowkan soldiers' uniforms echoes the color scheme of the film's prison. Here the obvious hand of visual design has been allowed to dictate the supposedly self-governing diegetic choices of Anderson's characters, giving them all the more the feeling of being specially collected pieces set inside a meticulously crafted curio cabinet. Anderson is aware of the strictures this imposes on the diegetic world of his films, and he acknowledges the degree to which his own characters are often held prisoner to his exacting aesthetic arrangements. Such is in fact the substance of what may arguably be one of the most profoundly self-aware inside jokes of Anderson's filmmaking. At the end of *Bottle Rocket*, when we see Dignan and the other inmates gathered in the prison yard in their uniforms, the backs of their jumpsuits read "Wasco State Penitentiary," evoking the last name of Anderson's production designer David Wasco and set decorator Sandy Reynolds-Wasco, a husband-and-wife team who worked with Anderson on his early films. Dignan—the most recognizably Andersonian character in this early film, what with his idiosyncratic haircut and jumpsuit and his penchant for planning overly elaborate criminal escapades in magic marker—has literally been made a prisoner of the film's production design team, the same figures who will a few years later entrap Max Fischer amid the boarding-school ephemera of Rushmore Academy and then sequester the Tenenbaum family in a house overflowing with eccentric clutter. Anderson's characters are collected objects too, so many visual pieces to be moved and arranged within his filmic tableau.

Anderson's Comedy

The absurdity of such arrangements, which visually and stylistically collapse the difference between Anderson's objects and his characters, is of course part of the point—and part of the comedy of Anderson's filmmaking. Though often born of pain and loss, the collector's enterprise, as a number of commentators have observed, frequently borders on the comedic and the absurd, and these elements of the collector's impulse are never lost on Anderson. On one level, the collection always encodes a kind of comedic social critique, an impulse, as Mark Graham writes, to "mock, invert, and disturb" (52) the socially assigned meaning and function of the objects collected and to make a kind of mockery of the very idea of functionality and usefulness themselves. On another level, though, the joke is always on the collector, in whose actions are inscribed what Rey Chow calls "the paradoxical movement . . . from the frivolous to the serious, from the casual pleasures of accumulating nonessential objects to the most perverse kinds of addiction," (286) a life given over to arranging and rearranging ephemera. Anderson's comedy works equally in both directions, as broad social critique and as trenchant self-criticism. His idiosyncratic filmic worlds can frequently read as a kind of joke on history and geography themselves, a frivolous rearrangement of the real wherein grand dramas featuring long-lost children, runaway lovers, or epochal wars unfold in what are essentially pastiche universes that "mock, invert, and disturb" their temporal referents, whether New York, New England, or Europe. Anderson is arguably one of the few directors of any epoch who can make the actual settings of his films comedic in and of themselves, enclosing his troubled characters within a townhouse cluttered to the point of absurdity or a scientific seagoing vessel that seems like something pulled out of a cartoon or a giant pastry puff of a hotel that everyone treats with the utmost seriousness and reverence. His filmic worlds teeter on the brink of the ridiculous and in so doing offer a kind of comedic reorientation of the known and the real, revealing the absurdity that is always "immanent to the existing world," to borrow Cheah's language of aesthetic world making (36).

At the same time that Anderson's collected worlds offer a comedic caricature of our known world, the enterprise of collection and the figure of the collector come under their own comedic scrutiny. For Anderson, the quest for order that is the collector's great impetus is inevitably an imperfect project, if not an absurdly impossible one. The very visual distance between his filmic worlds and our own—those five degrees of removal that he openly acknowledges—speak to the deep fantasy that is the collector's dream of order and arrangement, an aspiration that must be kept carefully sequestered from the real. Even here, though, the unordered and unpredictable manage to invade, elements exemplified in the sudden and often unexpected moments of slapstick that pervade all of Anderson's films: a priest taking a sudden tumble down a staircase in *The Royal Tenenbaums* or Zissou doing the same in *The Life Aquatic*; a madcap chase through a crowded train that ends with a character running into a plate glass window in *The Darjeeling Limited* or an elaborate toboggan race that ends with the villain being thrown from a cliff like Wile E. Coyote in *The Grand Budapest Hotel*; harmless car crashes in *Rushmore* and *Tenenbaums* or harmless lightning strikes in *Moonrise Kingdom*. Few directors since the days of Charlie Chaplin and Buster Keaton have included more pratfalls and frantic scrambles in their films alongside and in the midst of their more serious concerns. As funny as such moments are, they also are deeply jarring to the fantasies of orderly arrangement that Anderson's films otherwise try to project. For James MacDowell, the aesthetic punctuation that such slapstick moments present runs even stronger in Anderson's films than in other forms of comedy specifically because of the improbability of those moments within his filmic universe. Anderson's pratfalls, MacDowell writes, "surprise us with their suddenness and seeming inappropriateness in a manner not usually available to more conventional 'slapstick comedies' (which come with expectations that such gags will regularly occur)" (4). The consequences of these slapstick moments are almost always laughably negligible—a few bandages here, a temporarily charred face there—but the aesthetic disjunction is arguably severe. Slapstick is at heart an encounter with embodiment, with the inevitable indignities of being a body among bodies or a body among objects—that is to say, of living in the material world. Even in the realm of tight aesthetic control that marks Anderson's filmic worlds, the inescapability of our imperfect material condition remains.

In fact, such punctuated moments of slapstick often are among the only moments of emotional exuberance that Anderson ever allows within his films, which otherwise have become known for their distinctive form of comic muteness—what MacDowell calls an "understated style of deadpan" that is "dry, perfunctory, [and] excessively functional" (3), or what Vittrup terms the director's distinctively "mannerist movie worlds" (6). The humor here is one of basic incongruity, of a uniform manner of emotional address applied equally across nearly all situations regardless of fit. Anderson's standard comic mode is to approach the principle of comedic incongruity from a minimalist tack, to force his characters into underemotive responses to even maximally emotional situations, or as MacDowell writes, "to incongruously flatten, and in the process make dryly comic, a situation that could easily be treated as deeply dramatic" (4). From Zissou's declaration of his intention to devote his remaining life to finding and killing the shark that devoured his friend to Zero's litany of the tragedies that have befallen his family and his country, hardly any situation in Anderson's body of work appears to warrant a fully emotive response. Like nearly everything else in Anderson's filmic world, the emotional state of his characters is kept neatly ordered and controlled—in a word, collected.

And herein lies the most extensive aspect of comedic critique within Anderson's filmmaking. Exerting with few exceptions a preternatural emotional reserve, his characters embody the detachment and remove that is the darker side of the collector's idealistic world making, the extreme withdrawal into the self and the constant obsessions over order that are the markers of the trauma from which the collecting impulse emerges. They are nearly all, in their own ways, what Abbas calls "the traumatized, privatized, and impotent individual" (226) that marks the figure of the collector, and they are more often than not perfectly content to live their lives locked in various private worlds of their own making. If every collector also ultimately wishes to be collected, then the muffled uniformity of these characters' emotional lives speaks to the way that aspiration has been darkly fulfilled in the most isolating and stultifying of ways within Anderson's filmic universe. Describing Anderson's visual constructions, Rachel Joseph observes that "each framed moment in Anderson's films presents itself like a miniature stage pressed under glass and preserved as if it were some kind of childhood butterfly collection" (51). Only the butterflies here, the primary objects of display, are in fact the characters themselves, pinned in place and locked into their own isolated compartments, safely ensconced from each other and from the world. If their emotional lives seem strangely muted to us, it is because they are all living those lives under glass.

Anderson's Camera

In other words, Anderson's filmic worlds, in their objects and their persons alike, are ultimately designed for display—they call out for it. The collection always demands to be seen, and in fact the relationship between the objects of a collection and the gaze of the collector helps in large part to explain the highly recognizable cinematographic style that Anderson has developed for presenting his tightly crafted *mise-en-scène* and the tightly controlled figures that populate it. According to Stewart, a large part of the logic of a collection is manifested in the specific spatial logic of its physical arrangement and visual presentation:

> To ask which principles of organization are used in articulating the collection is to begin to discern what the collection is about. . . . The spatial organization of the collection, left to right, front to back, behind and before, depends upon the creation of an individual perceiving and apprehending the collection. . . . The space of the collection is a complex interplay of exposure and hiding, organization and the chaos of infinity. The collection relies upon the box, the cabinet, the cupboard, the seriality of shelves. (154, 157)

Stewart's directional explanation of the visual dynamics of the framed collection doubles as a trenchant description of Anderson's carefully controlled and almost obsessively geometric cinematography, his dedication to extreme frontality and cuts on 180- or 90-degree angles. Numerous commentators have noted the contrast between Anderson's maximalist rococo art design and his clear, unfussy cinematography, leading Seitz to call him "a fabulist who works in a borderline-minimalist vein" (238). Yet the cinematography in Anderson's films goes beyond any kind of simple minimalism to encompass a highly unique and immediately identifiable brand of direct presentationalism. (It is a cinematographic brand, moreover, that can be directly associated with Anderson's own visual eye to a greater extent than can be said of most directors, as Anderson typically develops "a shot list and an animatic containing stick figure representations of the desired framing and action" even before consulting with his long-time director of photography Robert Yeoman.)[7] More than letting us into the world of Anderson's films, his camera is displaying for us the contents of those filmic worlds much in the way one might show off a shelf of collectibles or open the door to a curio cabinet, an effect David Bordwell describes as images "that come to us boxed and bookended—tidy display cases preserving wildly untidy lives" ("Wes Anderson" 248).

The fundamental key to this effect is what Bordwell calls, in a word repurposed from art history, planimetric framing, a technique that relies on placing the camera in planes parallel or perpendicular to the defining physical features of the filmed environment. In Bordwell's description:

> "Planimetric" shooting involves framing people against a perpendicular background, as if they were taking part in a police lineup. Usually they face the camera, but you can rotate them ninety degrees to the left or right and show them to us in profile, or have them turn their backs to us. When filming groups, you can arrange the players in some depth, too, but again, they are stacked in perpendicular fashion, making each plane more or less parallel. ("Wes Anderson" 239)

It is this consistent geometric precision that gives Anderson's shots their notably rectilinear features, as though one has positioned oneself in front of a level shelf on which are held the contents of the filmic world. For Anderson, the technique is nearly always paired with an obvious attention to the symmetry or asymmetry of the frame, with most shots featuring the key subject or subjects notably positioned at the center of the frame (often carefully though improbably flanked by equivalent visual features on either side) or else notably off center such that deliberate attention is called to the negative space counterbalancing them. The total effect is to make Anderson's filmic worlds seem not just meticulously designed in their interiors but very carefully arranged in their presentations—and arranged specifically to be viewed from a single particular angle at which the camera obligingly positions us. *Here, look at my collection*, the director's camera seems to say, with each individual element meticulously presented in a symmetrical tableau or else paired with its equivalent pieces—unless such pieces are still missing from the collection, their space on the shelf reserved for them nonetheless. The implied hope is that those empty spaces might be filled in at a later time, Anderson's frame here formally redoubling the emotional ache that so many of his characters feel in searching for their own place within a larger collective or their own matched pieces within a fractured family or group.

This frontal-centric manner of framing is by no means unique to Anderson, but there are few directors who have used the style so consistently as the basic visual building block of their cinematic approach rather than as a technique to be employed for special emphasis. This goes back to the very beginnings of Anderson's career. The thirteen-minute black-and-white version of *Bottle Rocket* with which Anderson's filmmaking began is notable for the remarkable number of formally composed, front-on shots that stud the film. Though the technique had yet to become a defining aspect of his filmmaking, it is already at the very beginning of his career a dominant visual mode. In fact, as Anderson's attachment to planimetric framing began to grow over the course of his early films, he cultivated a specialized grammar of editing premised on a logic of preserving the frontal view, a visual system that is largely in place by *Rushmore*. (Again, the editing choices at work in Anderson's films tend to bear his direct fingerprints, the cuts within each scene being part of the animatic he develops in advance of shooting.) Anderson nearly always cuts along or at right angles to the so-called "180-degree line" that defines the implied center of the space within a shot, meaning that he utilizes shot/reverse shot sequences to cut across the 180-degree line, cuts through and parallel to the 180-degree line to move us further into or further out of the scene at hand without changing orientation, or else cuts to move us through the scene at hard right angles.[8] What for another director might be a special shot/reverse shot point of view sequence (which is the main purpose for which cutting across the 180-degree line is usually reserved) or else a highly elaborate and cinematographically distinctive cut at an unusual ninety-degree angle— these specialized techniques are for Anderson the core structures of his cinematic vocabulary. In other words, Anderson navigates through his filmic worlds in almost exactly the manner in which Stewart describes the viewer as regarding "the spatial organization of the collection, left to right, front to back, behind and before" (154). All Anderson's other main visual techniques are variants on the basic principles of frontal framing and of editing at angles of ninety degrees: behind, in front, to the left, to the right. Anderson has become famous for panning according to this same visual logic, moving the camera steadily and slowly left and right, forward and backward, or up and down across the rectilinear worlds of his films—a technique that is especially notable when paired with the elaborate dollhouse-style cutaways that he first created for the cross-section visual of the *Belafonte* in *The Life Aquatic* (fig. 6) and then used to similarly striking effect with the railroad cars at the end of *The Darjeeling Limited* or the Bishop home in *Moonrise Kingdom*. Yet here Anderson is merely achieving through camera movement within the frame what he normally accomplishes through cutting between frames:

Figure 6. Introducing the *Belafonte*

a kind of careful, point-by-point navigation across the filmic world that takes us piece by piece through the parts of the collection. On occasion (and more frequently than most directors), Anderson will tilt his camera up or down according to the same visual logic, showing us what is above or below as opposed to left or right. Though there are occasional flashes of three-quarter views for emphasis—an inversion of standard cinematographic practice wherein such framing is the norm and the formal, symmetrical shots of Anderson's world are the exception—for the most part Anderson's camera forces the spectator into a position of formal, removed viewership. Through Anderson's frame, Bordwell argues, his cinematic world "gains a layer of formality, almost ceremony" ("Wes Anderson" 238) that yields an occasionally disconcerting level of emotional distance, turning his characters "into toy people" (240). *Here is my collection*, his camera seems to say. *Let me show you all the parts* (fig. 7).

Of course, the recursive irony in this technique is that the cinematographic style Anderson so carefully developed to display the components of his collected *mise-en-scène* is itself a kind of pristine collection of antiquated cinematic techniques. It is a collection of formal tools that is highly unique in today's cinematic landscape, not to be confused with the equally prevalent collection of interfilmic references that mark Anderson's cinema. It is true enough that Anderson, like many a cinephile film director, has created in his body of work a kind of special library of filmic references and influences, which is a collection of a sort. He openly cites the influence of François Truffaut's *400 Blows* on his own

Figure 7. Anderson displays the parts of his collection

boarding-school drama *Rushmore*, for instance, whereas *The Royal Tenenbaums* was conceived in the image of Orson Welles's *The Magnificent Ambersons*, whose famous grand mansion the Tenenbaum townhouse was supposed to specifically invoke.[9] Likewise, Anderson's 2008 commercial for SoftBank, starring a bumbling but painstakingly polite Brad Pitt in a ridiculous banana-yellow getup with matching yellow hat is a more or less explicit riff on the films of Jacques Tati (themselves derivative of Charlie Chaplin's films), and his gloss on the behind-the-scenes filmmaking process for his 2006 commercial for American Express deliberately calls to mind Truffaut's *Day for Night*.

Yet on the level of specific technique, Anderson's filmmaking goes far beyond the kind of film-to-film references that are common to any cinematically literate director. Rather, his cinematic toolbox—the array of actual filmmaking tactics that he employs—is like that of a car mechanic stricken by collectomania who uses only tools preserved from past golden ages of the automotive industry even though he works on modern automobiles. Take Anderson's commitment to the planimetric frame. As a technique of emphasis, this style of framing remains in use, but it has not been widely applied as a common mode of cinematic craftsmanship since the early days of silent film, roughly "the first ten years of film's development" in Browning's estimation, during which time it provided "an evolutionary link with the theatre" (146). It is today relegated to what Bordwell calls a "novice" technique, one that is typically trained out of a director in film school ("Wes Anderson" 241).[10] It abounds only in films that predate the development of continuity editing associated with the work of D. W. Griffith in the late 1900s and mid 1910s—largely because, in the absence of continuity editing's powerful techniques of emphasis and directed attention, extreme frontality affords a ready means of guiding the viewer's eye across the screen and ensuring that key points of narrative or visual information are quickly communicated. This is part of what Bordwell refers to in *On the History of Film Style* as "the long-take, 'scenic' method" (198) of film construction wherein "the resources of set design, aperture framing, and figure movement" are used to create "highly functional staging patterns" that occlude the need for frequent cutting (185). For those versed in this period of early silent filmmaking, Anderson's shot composition structure cannot help but recall the mainstay techniques of this preclassical era, so much so that Browning has dubbed Anderson a kind of latter-day "king of the silent screen" (143).

But Anderson's formalist cinephilia goes far beyond a single manner of framing and presentation. Just as Anderson's means of presenting cinematic space recalls techniques associated with the early years of cinema, so too do his means of navigating through that space. As Charlie Keil has explored at length, early cinematic narrative—particularly during the important "transitionary phase" between around 1908 and 1913—depended on a logic of "proximate" or "contiguous" spaces, using adjoining or coterminous structures around which the narrative could be built so as to diegetically justify within the frame cuts between locations, which were taken to be logically taxing on viewers before Griffith helped to broadly popularize their usage (Keil 108, 109). Early filmmakers, Keil records, were inordinately concerned with the ways in which "any act of cutting from an established space can risk producing spectatorial confusion" and thus afforded particular attention to demarcating "the spatial status of each individual shot" (105, 106). Anderson's forward-to-backward and side-to-side manner of editing across rectilinear spaces directly recalls the stilted, geometrically determined compositions of the epoch before the age of classical consolidation and its decoupling of diegetic space and cinematic style. Even the dollhouse-style room-to-room editing of Anderson's filmmaking is a kind of transposition from the earliest years of cinema. As Barry Salt has observed, the preponderance of early films set in the domestic sphere, comedies especially, consisted of an incessant visual monotony of "room-to-room movement in side-by-side spaces filmed from the front" (38). Anderson has taken this long-abandoned compositional structure as a kind of direct inheritance.

Yet as a collector of old cinematic techniques, Anderson is by no means limited to the early silent era. Just like the true collector of Benjamin's description, he pays no heed to temporality or historicity and instead picks and chooses those techniques that suit his fancy—the cinematic equivalent of placing the Jacobean chairs next to the Sheraton cabinets. From the obvious to the invisible, the prominent to the peripheral, Anderson's formal toolbox is filled with borrowed and reappropriated antiquarian filmmaking tactics. His famous tracking shots with their elaborate sequences of carefully framed, through-the-dollhouse-window perspectives on character and scene are to the cinema historian a direct appropriation from the work of Max Ophüls, so much so that Tyree pointedly refers to this supposedly trademark technique of Anderson's filmmaking as his "Ophülsian tracking shot" (24)—a debt Anderson has more or less openly acknowledged in his listing of Ophüls's *The Earrings of Madame de . . .* as his favorite Criterion Collection title on the company's website. Likewise the abundant use of on-screen titling that has become another hallmark of Anderson's filmmaking, which is acknowledged by the director as a direct borrowing from Jean-Luc Godard and his use of the technique in films like *A Woman Is a Woman* and *The Chinese*. In Anderson's words, "The guy I always thought of as the one who puts the words on the screen is Godard—those movies are just filled with words" (qtd. in Seitz 88). Even the visual structure of Anderson's on-screen text acknowledges a degree of borrowing in his famous utilization of the Futura font, which appears in the title sequences of all his films from *Bottle Rocket* to *Fantastic Mr. Fox*, as well as in nearly every instance of diegetic print within those films. The text type was at one point so ubiquitous in Anderson's work that it became known by some as "the Wes Anderson font," yet it might as easily be called the "Stanley Kubrick font," in that Kubrick likewise had a stated affinity for the typeface and used it prominently in six out of his thirteen films.[11] "I think I'm always pretty influenced by Kubrick," Anderson acknowledges (Gilchrist).

Anderson's rehabilitation of faded or forgotten cinematic technique is equally prevalent in the subtler aspects of his filmmaking. Since *Rushmore*, for instance, he has filmed nearly all his movies in anamorphic widescreen using a Panavision Primo 40mm Anamorphic lens. Although the 2.35 anamorphic widescreen ratio is still in use today, it is dwarfed by the ubiquity of the 1.85 aspect ratio in which most films are shot and according to which nearly all contemporary movie theater screens are built. Producing a slight cylindrical distortion in the frame, the use of anamorphic widescreen is instantly if imperceptibly noticeable; Anderson's trademark use of the format harkens back to its heyday in the CinemaScope and Panavision craze of the 1960s and 1970s, when it was the standard film format for epic filmmaking. On top of that, his use of the Panavision 40mm anamorphic lens in particular holds a special pedigree, it being the preferred lens of Roman Polanski and the one through which the whole of *Chinatown* was filmed. (Anderson has long acknowledged Polanski as another major influence on the order of Kubrick.)[12] Similarly, Anderson has made a point of often using antique film stocks in his cinematography. Although he is among a small coterie of modern directors who still work only with analog film, Anderson is relatively unique in his special interest in the history of his film stocks. For *The Life Aquatic*, for example, he employed Ektachrome reversal stock that has been largely out of use for decades but was once the standard film stock of *National Geographic*. In *Moonrise Kingdom*, he used a period-appropriate Super 16mm film to give the picture the look of 1960s-era Kodachrome. Anderson also has experimented with rehabilitating antiquated aspect ratios within his films, shooting each temporal section of *The Grand Budapest Hotel*, for instance, in a different, historically appropriate ratio: a Hollywood-standard 1.85 aspect ratio for those portions of the film set in the present day and a letterboxed version of the same for those portions set in 1985, reminiscent of how a film might appear cropped when shown on television; his typical 1960s-reminiscent 2.35:1 widescreen aspect ratio for the portion of the film set in 1968; and for the longest portions of the film a truly anachronistic 1.33 aspect ratio (technically 1.37:1)—the famed "Academy ratio" that was declared the film industry standard by the Academy of Motion Picture Arts and Sciences in 1932, the same year in which *Grand Budapest* is set.[13] Rendered obsolete by the widescreen revolution in 1953, the Academy ratio has been used on only the rarest occasions in the intervening decades. (Michel Hazanavicius's *The Artist*, conceived as a kind of museum piece paean to the era of silent filmmaking, is one of the few other prominent contemporary films to use the Academy ratio.)

Anderson's commitment to using historically laden film stocks and aspect ratios undoubtedly produces subtle effects on the viewer, but perhaps the most notable aspect of his formal antiquarianism lies in his commitment to bygone special effects techniques and other similarly outmoded means of achieving relatively simple visual ends. In *The Life Aquatic*, for example, Anderson insisted that all the fabulous marine creatures featured in the film be created using stop-motion animation techniques and employed to that end the famous stop-motion animator Henry Selick. Stop-motion animation—the oldest of all animation techniques, dating back to 1899—has been enjoying a renaissance of sorts since at least the 1990s as a particularly artful form of feature-length animated filmmaking (a tradition in which Anderson's own animated *Fantastic Mr. Fox* figures prominently), but it has not been widely used as a mainstream tool for special effects creation since the 1980s. To craft via stop motion such creatures as the crayon ponyfish or the jaguar shark—which Anderson claims to be the largest stop-motion puppet ever created for a film—is inevitably to hearken back to the days of renowned model animators like Ray Harryhausen or Willis O'Brien and the special-effects creatures of films like *The 7th Voyage of Sinbad* or *The Lost World*.[14] More unique still is Anderson's decision to use model animation to create the flooding scenes in *Moonrise Kingdom* and many of the Alpine sequences in *The Grand Budapest Hotel*, employing a technique that by his own admission "feels fake," but one that evokes a kind of midcentury aesthetic of cinematic spectacle. The point, Anderson claims, was that the sequence "feels fake as a miniature, rather than fake as a computer" (qtd. in Seitz 306). Or, as he put it in another interview, "The particular brand of artificiality that I like to use is an old-fashioned one" (qtd. in Murphy). One imagines a similar rationale for Anderson's decision to use a kind of split-screen technique straight out of classical Hollywood for the telephone conversations in *Moonrise Kingdom*, wherein each half of the evenly divided screen depicts a party in conversation, like something out of *Pillow Talk* (fig. 8). Yet sometimes Anderson's antiquarian techniques are, by design, hardly noticeable at all. Anderson is, for instance, a great proponent of using forced perspective in the creation of his film sets, allowing him to engage in "the challenge of getting it in the camera" (qtd. in Seitz 244), without having to add anything in postproduction. The precarious tree house in *Moonrise Kingdom*, teetering high above the khaki scout camp, was built on location at half scale, whereas much of the perceived depth in *Fantastic Mr. Fox* was achieved using differently scaled versions of the main characters and set-pieces (fig. 9). By the same token, Anderson created actual theatrical curtains to open and close between the different acts of *Rushmore*, building them at a reduced scale and filming them in camera rather than adding them in postproduction. These kinds of practical special-effects techniques executed directly on set and captured on film without digital enhancement or alteration have not been widely used in decades—even to the point of being effectively obsolete in the case of on-set, live-action forced perspective. Anderson claims the appeal to be one of creating "a handmade feeling" and has even expressed some interest in experimenting with doing "a fade to black or an iris shot in the camera," (qtd. in Seitz 244), revisiting complicated silent-era means of achieving what are now quite simple effects.

Figure 8. Split screen in *Moonrise Kingdom*

Figure 9. Half-scale forced perspective in
Moonrise Kingdom

In other words, Anderson approaches the very craft of filmmaking as a kind of collector, selecting out particular techniques or specific formal strategies from across the history of cinema that he will isolate and recombine into the unique concoction that is his own brand of late-twentieth and early twenty-first-century filmmaking. The underlying impulse to acknowledge and pay homage to film history is in some ways a common one among contemporary filmmakers, even if Anderson's particular brand of cinematographic collectomania is rather unique. Bordwell calls it the problem of "belatedness," a condition in which, "after the early 1960s, most filmmakers became painfully aware of working in the shadow of enduring monuments" (*The Way Hollywood Tells It* 25–26). The question of originality becomes a driving one among the cinematically literate directors of the later twentieth century, even more so for those, like Anderson, whose careers began in the shadow of 1960s and 1970s New Hollywood. "The more you know, the more you understand the gap that separates you from the great tradition, and the more you fret about what you can contribute," Bordwell writes (*The Way Hollywood Tells It* 23). For most directors, this anxiety leads primarily to a condition of allusionism and cinephilia, which in turn has reinforced a specialist film culture "that demands film references as part of the pleasures of moviegoing" (Bordwell, *The Way Hollywood*

Tells It 25). Anderson's appropriation of the actual formal techniques of filmmaking eras gone by is something else again and is a response to the condition of belatedness that is largely unique to him. More than an attempt to reference or visually remix the past, it is an attempt to build a tangible connection to filmmaking worlds now lost, emblematic of what Chow calls the collector's imperative to establish "an intimate, albeit outmoded, relationship with the past through its remnants" (294). It is not that Anderson's cinema represents a vast storehouse of antiquated technique or a museum-minded replication of filmmaking procedures from a certain period of time; neither are his films composed in explicit homage to a particular epoch of cinema or in imitation of a specific filmmaking style or genre. Rather, like the true collector, Anderson has assembled an assortment of individual antiquarian techniques that he has wholly separated from context and from time, replacing "history . . . with order beyond the realm of temporality," in Stewart's phrase (151). Obviously the techniques are not beyond functionality—indeed, they are all still useful to Anderson in his filmmaking, making him the rare collector who actually puts his collection to work. But his engagement with and utilization of the outmoded is in the manner of the car collector who insists on driving his classic automobiles around town, the rare book collector who actually reads his first editions, or the music collector who listens to everything on vinyl. Ultimately, utility is not the operative concern. Rather, building on what Chow observes of such collectors, "the interest of collecting lies in the impossibility of disentangling it from *re*collection, from an attempt to reassemble the past" according to the prerogative of the collector (294; emphasis in the original). Anderson has taken this assemblage of formal techniques and combined them together into a Benjaminian "magic circle" of new meanings, harnessing them as expressions of a personal visual perspective that draws from each individual element but is tied to none of them.

In this way, Anderson's catalog of cinematographic technique offers a kind of highly idiosyncratic tour through the history of cinema, not unlike the way in which the soundtracks to his films—carefully coordinated with the assistance of music supervisor Randall Poster—are often described as presenting an eclectic take on popular music of the twentieth century. Anderson is perhaps best known for his affinity for the music of the British Invasion, which features most heavily in the

Rushmore soundtrack, but in fact his distinctive musical choices run the gamut of twentieth-century genres and forms and include such rarities as the Sonny Rollins tune prominently used in the original short of *Bottle Rocket*, the Hank Williams songs scattered liberally throughout *Moonrise Kingdom*, the operatic, choral, and orchestral works of Benjamin Britten used in that same film, the ballads of French crooner Joe Dassin in *The Darjeeling Limited*, the 1990s-era indie rock number by Elliott Smith in *The Royal Tenenbaums*, and musical pieces actually pulled from the soundtracks of other films, as in the portions of the scores from Satyajit Ray and Merchant-Ivory films utilized in *The Darjeeling Limited*. Anderson's musical choices, as much as his set design and *mise-en-scène*, are frequently described as eclectic, offering "a soup of different pop, rock, and classical music" (Hubbert 308), reflecting the degree to which his collector's prerogative admits of no logic other than its own internally generated motivations. The same goes for Anderson's propensity to include a bookshelf's worth of idiosyncratic literary allusions within his films, outlining an eccentric library of classic and obscure titles to be placed alongside his eclectic music catalog. These include his direct and semidirect adaptations of the works of Roald Dahl and Stefan Zweig, his debt to J. D. Salinger's *Franny and Zooey* in conceiving his adolescent worlds, the influence of children's novels like E. L. Konigsburg's *From the Mixed-up Files of Mrs. Basil E. Frankweiler* and Helen Cressweel's *Bagthorpe Saga*, as well as broad thematic inheritances from writers ranging from E. M. Forster to Herman Melville.[15] His approach to cinematic history is much the same, both as catholic and as personalized: silent-era framing mixed with 1960s-era anamorphic ratios mixed with midcentury practical effects, which, although each individually has its own historicity, when taken all together can only be described as the Anderson style.

Were Anderson making films in the shadow of a coherent cinematic monoculture—were he a Josef von Sternberg trying to execute a unique cinematographic vision within the classical studio system or a Charlie Chaplin making his films just next door to but outside the reach of the big Hollywood studios—this collector's aesthetic that he has so carefully cultivated might in some way be subversive. But as a filmmaker working at the end of the twentieth century and the beginning of the twenty-first, it can be viewed only in the context of loss and displacement, an imperfect restorative measure, an attempt to carry on. Anderson has not so much raided the museum of cinema history as he has picked up whatever he could carry after the looting was already finished so that he could at least try to make something new. Gilles Deleuze, in his monumental *Cinema 1* and *Cinema 2*, specifically describes the breakdown of the studio system and the end of the dominance of the classical style it helped enforce as a kind of desultory moment arising from the literal destruction of World War II. That conflict, Deleuze writes, "greatly increased the situations which we no longer know how to react to, in spaces which we no longer know how to describe" (*Cinema 2* xi) such that cinematic culture "could only be reconstituted following a broken line lifted from among all the points and all the lines of the whole" (*Cinema 1* 205). The classical style would not be immediately vanquished, but the paradigm shift that would eventually take place, which Deleuze describes as being that from the movement-image based in sequence and action of *Cinema 1* to the time-image based in simultaneity and reflection of *Cinema 2*, would be profound. We can only assume that Anderson's cinephilia, which predates and presumably led to his desire to become a film director, is deeply felt—witness the somewhat comical lengths to which he went merely to get a response to his filmmaking from a gatekeeper like Pauline Kael. Anderson draws his influences widely, ranking Orson Welles and *Peanuts* animator Bill Meléndez and Satyajit Ray and *Star Wars* all as being important to his formation as a director, and he seems intuitively to understand the history of cinema as being one of diffusion and dispersal. His response is to collect, to create an order of his own in the absence of any larger governing order. As Benjamin observed, "Right from the start, the great collector is struck by the confusion, by the scatter, in which the things of the world are found" (*Arcades* 211). Anderson's body of films functions as a kind of eclectic sanctuary wherein techniques long forgotten, tactics now outdated, and stylistic elements considered passé can recombine into something new and energizing and powerful. But of course they are not just stylistic exercises, cinematic études that celebrate form as an end in itself. They are rich cinematic worlds—packed with characters battling the same encroaching forces of disorder and the same traumatized response to loss that Anderson's own filmmaking represents. They are films about collectors, yes, but more than that they are films about people who are seeking to be collected, looking for a place or a person through which they can find a way back to themselves, hoping that after all that has been lost there is still something that can be recovered.

The Contents of the Curio Cabinet

Shelf 1: Anderson's Family Heirlooms

The Royal Tenenbaums (2001)   The dynamic of loss and recovery enacted through the processes of collecting and the desire to be collected is perhaps nowhere clearer in Anderson's filmmaking than in *The Royal Tenenbaums*, which for many Anderson fans and commentators is a kind of ur-text of the Andersonian canon. It is the film, in other words, that for most moviegoers was the earliest and clearest statement of who Anderson would be as a filmmaker. In Seitz's words, "All the stylistic tics that Anderson developed in *Rushmore* bloom rather explosively here, like irradiated sci-fi flowers" (110). Although many of Anderson's defining stylistic characteristics and much of his thematic focus can, in retrospect, be seen in his two earlier films, *Bottle Rocket* and *Rushmore*, neither of those two efforts falls easily or entirely inside the scope of what would become Anderson's defining traits. *Bottle Rocket* shows a deep interest in issues of collecting and collection in relationship to the breakdown and reformation of family units or similar collective groups, but it also owes much to the talky, self-consciously quirky crime capers of 1990s independent cinema—a kind of "Reservoir Geeks" in the words of the marketing copy for the 1996 DVD release. *Rushmore*, although beloved of many of Anderson's fans (in Seitz's words, "There are few perfect films; *Rushmore* is one of them" [71]), is like a kind of later Anderson movie in embryo, showing signs of the director's future developments but presenting none of them in full maturation. In *Tenenbaums*, all the nascent hallmarks in *Rushmore* would come into efflorescence. The planimetric framing that was a clear visual leitmotif of the earlier film would rise to the level of prevailing visual style. The idiosyncratic visual appearance and nearly hermetic self-absorption of *Rushmore*'s central hero would spread to define nearly every character in *Tenenbaums*. The meticulous visual design of certain scenes in *Rushmore*—Max's imagined corner of scholarly repose in his imagined mathematics classroom; Edward Appleby's cluttered childhood room, where Max and Rosemary have a key confrontation; the entire visual world of Max's scenographically elaborate but emotionally adolescent plays—these elements would spread across Anderson's diegetic world until they formed its entirety. Even the distinctive and sometimes startling musical choices of the earlier film, which had a clear organizing logic of British Invasion rock, would grow into the eclectic unpredictability of the *Tenenbaums* soundtrack, perhaps the only album on which Maurice Ravel and the Ramones can be found side by side. In fact, the degree to which *Tenenbaums* is taken to be definitive to Anderson's style is so great that it is not uncommon to find elements that appeared only later in the director's work to be misremembered backward into that film, as in the not uncommon misconception that the famed Tenenbaums townhouse is presented in the same kind of dollhouse-style tracking shot that would first appear in *The Life Aquatic*.[16]

If *Tenenbaums* is central to Anderson's aesthetic overall, it also is more specifically the central entry in one of three thematic subgroups into which Anderson's body of eight films can be divided according to the particular logic of collection and belonging that they explore. Insofar as Anderson's films are fundamentally about the search for a place of belonging and the promises of order and arrangement that such a place can hold against the traumatic dispersion of the wider world, then that promised place of admission and acceptance—the collection into which Anderson's eccentric isolates can be sorted—comes in three varieties. There is the family, which, though often broken, can attempt to be reformed in some way; there are the surrogate families, which attempt to replace and stand for families that can no longer or never were able to cohere; and there are the pairings and partnerships, romantic or professional, that can obviate the need for any wider group. *The Royal Tenenbaums* is the first of Anderson's films to deal explicitly with the dynamics of the family and to explore the ways that this original collection into which we are all first sorted can be broken apart and put back together. It is in this sense the most autobiographical of Anderson's films, even as it is among the most fanciful. Although *Rushmore* is very loosely based on Anderson's experiences at a tony Houston-area private school (and was in fact shot at the very school that Anderson attended), its central emotional trauma of premature parental death is, for Anderson, an imagined one—and arguably a displacement of the actual familial trauma that he has described as defining his childhood, that being the divorce of his parents when he was eight years old. That divorce was, in Anderson's recollection, "the most crucial event of my brothers and my growing up" (qtd. in "Wes Anderson: Hollywood's New King of Comedy"). *The Royal Tenenbaums* is the story of a fractured family riven by a decades-long parental separation, a family desperately attempting, with perhaps predictably disastrous results, to cleave itself back together. Or, put another way, it is a story about characters beset by a trauma that they do not so much try to heal as to simply undo, a course of action that is as understandable as it is outrageous.

This idea of an unhealed trauma lingering over every character in the film helps explain in large part the obsessive focus on collections and collecting in the picture, a level of explicit engagement with the visuality and emotional dynamics of collecting that far exceeds any of Anderson's other works. Every single member of the Tenenbaum household is identified in some way as a collector, and many are in large part defined, visually or narratively, through the nature and breadth of their collections. Margot (Gwyneth Paltrow), befitting her status as a fantastically precocious playwright who received her first major grant in the ninth grade, boasts a capacious "library of plays" (the screenplay says it numbers in the thousands; fig. 10), and her business-minded brother Chas (Ben Stiller) is pictured in his opening moments with a collection of ties that would be the envy of any Wall Street financier—what seem to be hundreds of them are arranged meticulously in his boyhood closet. Only Richie (Luke Wilson), who will emerge later as a professional tennis star, has a series of collections befitting a normal childhood: a series of pinned butterflies in shadow boxes attached to his bedroom door and coordinated sets of matchbox cars that appear very carefully arranged in the corners of Anderson's frame throughout the film. The adults of Anderson's world are equally besotted of collecting. There are the George Caitlin prints that decorate Etheline's (Anjelica Huston) office, and aspiring Tenenbaum family member Eli Cash's (Owen Wilson) full cycle of Miguel Calderón paintings (not to mention a sizable collection of pornographic videos featured very prominently in one shot in his apartment). Royal Tenenbaum's one question of the hotel management at the Lindbergh Palace Hotel when he learns he has been expelled

LIBRARY OF PLAYS

Figure 10. Margot's personal library

from the suite in which he has been living for years is "Where's my encyclopedias?"; they will reappear later in the film as the sole remaining possession he bequeaths to his family. Only those most outside the Tenenbaum orbit—Margot's husband Raleigh St. Clair (Bill Murray) and Etheline's suitor Henry Sherman (Danny Glover)—are exempted from this omnipresent collectomania.

Individually, and in their own ways, the members of the Tenenbaum clan (and those who wish for honorary entry like Eli, who spent his college years sending his grades to Etheline and continues to send his professional press clippings to her) are trying to create worlds of abundant order and sense in counterpoint to the maelstrom of anguish and hurt that is as much a defining feature of the towering Tenenbaum townhome as its eclectic furnishings. No one can imagine that Royal ever made a loving or attentive father or that the Tenenbaum household was a place of emotional tranquility: Anderson's narrator (Alec Baldwin) informs us of the ways that Royal embezzled money from his business-minded son, openly put down young Margot's early dramatic efforts, and made no secret of his explicit favoritism toward Richie, to say nothing of his numerous extramarital affairs. Anderson's storyline begins, after a lengthy narrated prologue, in what amounts to the Tenenbaum family's attempt to circumscribe this emotional turmoil by way of a parental separation. "We had to make certain sacrifices as a result of having children," Royal (Gene Hackman) tells the assembled kids, in what may be one of the most spectacularly wrongheaded announcements of parental discord in the history of modern divorce. Twenty-two years later, the separation still stands, the

Tenenbaum household having never resolved either into reconciliation or formal division. Rather than stanching the emotional hemorrhaging of their tempestuous family life, the separation of the Tenenbaum parents merely froze that wound in place, rendering the trauma of that one family meeting with Royal as alive for the Tenenbaum children in their maturity as it was in the moment of their preadolescence. For all their outrageous accomplishments later in childhood and into adolescence and young adulthood—writing Broadway plays, becoming titans of business and finance, winning professional Grand Slam tennis competitions—the adult Tenenbaum children essentially seem suspended in time in the moment at which their family came apart, the visual presentation of the three children in that fateful early scene meant to deliberately evoke their adulthood selves in miniature. *Sic transit gloria*—glory fades—as Max Fischer wistfully reminds us multiple times throughout *Rushmore*. It could be a kind of advance warning issued to the preternaturally accomplished Tenenbaum children still to come, though usually glory does not fade quite so quickly as it did for these three young virtuosi. By early adulthood all have seen their careers and public profiles slip away or severely diminish. "Virtually all memory of the brilliance of the young Tenenbaums had been erased by two decades of betrayal, failure, and disaster," as the narrator says. One gets the distinct impression that their many successes amounted to just so many attempts to soothe the ache of that internal family collapse with excessive levels of external validation, each career essentially abandoned or thrown away—quite literally in the case of Richie's spectacularly blown tennis match—when the emotional salve no longer worked.

It is not the collapse of these glorious careers, however, that hastens the Tenenbaums' adulthood retreat back to their childhood home. Rather, it is the failure to find some other unit of belonging that can substitute for the troubled family from which they all came, a new collective to take the place of the one that was taken apart in their youth. Margot is the first to undertake this search for a possible new home, her own position in the Tenenbaum claim being the most tenuous—Royal, as the film's narrator notes, makes a point of always introducing her, thoughtlessly and self-servingly, as his "adopted daughter, Margot Tenenbaum." Placed on a slightly separate tier from the other Tenenbaums, Margot started early in life looking for an alternate place of belonging—seeking it at one point in an attempted reunion with her birth family in the backwoods of Indiana and at another by camping out at the fictional Public Archives, a whimsical rendering of New York's Museum of Natural History, whose famous taxidermy halls, recreated briefly in the film as Margot's newly adopted home with her brother Richie, are the *sine qua non* example of the lived world rendered as a series of collected objects carefully displayed. Neither adventure lasts, and so at the age of nineteen Margot abandons her playwriting career entirely to pursue a series of adult relationships—a nine-day marriage to a Jamaican reggae artist, multiple amorous affairs, and finally a loveless marriage to the neurologist and author Raleigh St. Clair. As if in counterpoint to Margot's abundance of attempted familial and romantic groupings, Richie seeks to isolate himself entirely after abandoning his tennis career, rendering himself beholden to no place, time, or group. He spends his days traveling alone on a luxury ocean liner, on which he "had seen both poles, five oceans, the Amazon, and the Nile." Unaligned to anyone or anything and entirely unreachable except by onboard radio, he strives to make himself immune to all possible attachments beyond the original family grouping from which he has broken; even on board his ship at sea he wears essentially the same outfit that he did in that family meeting with his father, only now his tennis shirt is covered by a camel-hair blazer. Among the Tenenbaum children, Chas alone makes an effort to start over and create a lasting new familial grouping—only to see his new nuclear family torn apart when his wife is killed in a plane crash that the other family members all survive. Chas's traumatized response is to literally regroup. Eschewing the businessman's suits that defined his costuming prior to the crash, Chas begins to dress himself and his two sons in identical red Adidas tracksuits, giving them the disconcerting appearance of being matched collectible dolls and making it as visually clear as possible that they are part of the same group. But even this is not enough to placate the loss that he suffers under. Citing trumped-up claims of insufficient safety systems in place at the high-end apartment building where he lives with his children, he moves what remains of his family back into the dilapidated home where he spent his childhood—even into the same room, where he and his sons now sleep together. Margot soon follows ("Why are they allowed to do that?" she says upon learning that Chas and the boys have returned home), and after her, Richie. Each in turn, like Benjamin's figure of the collector, has been "struck by the confusion, by the scatter, in which the things of the world are found" (*Arcades* 211). Facing a world of traumatic accidents, loveless pairings, and aimless wandering, the Tenenbaum children return themselves to the same location they were once so adamant about escaping, seeking to force back into being the collection, troubled as it was, where they felt they first (and perhaps best) belonged. It is a dynamic that is diegetically redoubled within the film, when Richie, almost immediately upon returning home, makes the impulsive decision to release his pet falcon Mordecai, only to find that the falcon later returns on his own, his feathers now turned newly white—a sign, Richie claims, of having undergone a traumatic experience.

Anderson leaves no doubt that this is a troubled emotional regression rather than a happy family reunion, a symptom of collection as a potentially dangerous retreat from the disorder and discomfort of the world. The Tenenbaum household and the childhood it represents is a trap for these grown children, a point that Anderson visually emphasizes in multiple scenes set within a particularly small closet in the house where various characters retreat to share secret communications surrounded on all sides by what seem like hundreds of old children's board games stacked like so many bricks in a prison wall (fig. 11). Here the idea of the collection is rendered as a kind of obsessive overcompensation, one that can entrap its creators in its totalizing logic of order and arrangement. Indeed, the longer the Tenenbaum children spend in their childhood home, the smaller and smaller their worlds become. Chas, once a successful businessman, relocates a kind of skeleton crew of associates and assistants into the same room from which he once ran his childhood business breeding and selling Dalmatian mice, leading one to wonder whether he ever in fact leaves the house at all anymore. Richie eventually relocates from his boyhood bedroom to a children's camping tent pitched in the middle of the living room, meticulously decorated with childhood artifacts, entrapping himself within a subsection of a subsection of his childhood world. There is, ironically, a globe featured prominently in the tent reminiscent of his former world travels, but it is the world abstracted and held at a significant remove—a child's toy that lights up from the inside. And Margot, who has taken lovers across the world and remains married to a world-famous neurologist and author, takes to sleeping with Eli, who grew up across the street, almost literally the boy next door.

Figure 11. Confrontation in the game closet |

The great Tenenbaum children, who once seemed to hold the worlds of business, culture, and sport at their fingertips, have now retreated as far from those worlds and as far from their own adulthoods as they possibly can, back into the closest thing to a world of order and arrangement that they ever knew. And just as Royal Tenenbaum played a central role in originally tearing that world apart, so too does he play a central and no less destructive role in trying to cobble it back together. The impetus behind Royal's return to the family homestead—achieved by way of a concocted diagnosis of terminal stomach cancer to win the family's sympathy—is ostensibly Henry's proposal of marriage to Etheline, one of many that she has received over the years but the first that she has seriously entertained. Yet the stakes actually go much deeper than a rival's bid for the affections of a woman Royal has been separated from for twenty-two years. Royal's greatest interest is not so much in protecting his romantic relationship as in policing the boundaries of the Tenenbaum family unit. He believes himself to be the organizing intelligence of the eclectic collection that is the Tenenbaums and the one in charge of determining the appropriate components it may contain. This is a privilege he made abundantly clear in Margot's childhood in his idiosyncratic and hurtful insistence on always noting her adopted status, and it is a privilege he continues to exercise by repeatedly and seemingly willfully forgetting the existence of Chas's deceased wife. He is the collector of the Tenenbaums collection, and it is up to him to acquire or deaccession new components. He will ignore those he does not want, and he will seek out those he does—as when he surreptitiously forces a relationship with his grandchildren Ari (Grant Rosenmeyer) and Uzi (Jonah Meyerson) against Chas's stated wishes or when he commands Etheline to take back their family servant Pagoda (Kumar Pallana) after she has cast him out of the house for helping Royal in his schemes. Royal holds himself to some extent outside the Tenenbaum collection he has assembled, engaging in numerous affairs that flaunt the boundaries and loyalties of the clan and even punishing Chas during a childhood game of BB guns with a surprise shot from behind for making the mistake of believing that he and Royal could ever actually be on the same team. "There are no teams," Royal informs him, at least not where Royal himself is concerned. Royal even says directly in the film that he does not consider himself a Tenenbaum, responding "Me too" when Eli laments that he "always wanted to be a Tenenbaum." Although ostensibly a reference to his long exile from the family homestead, Royal's comment also sets him deliberately outside the collection that he has amassed and that he still believes he controls. He cannot *be* a Tenenbaum, because he is the one who curates the Tenenbaums. The members of his own family are for Royal not his kin to whom he owes responsibilities but simply external expressions of himself, just as any collector's prized items are a material expression of his self in the world. To him, they are all, as Anderson's title makes clear, Royal Tenenbaums.

For Anderson, this attempt on Royal's part to project his own identity in and through the family members around him, even and especially after they have outright rejected him, is undoubtedly a kind of sickness. Hence the ugliness of Royal's conflict with Henry, which involves not only a poor impersonation of someone dying of the same cancer from which Henry's first wife suffered but also a remarkably undisguised racism, which escalates from muttered references to "lay it on me" to a scene in which Royal calls his rival "Coltrane" in order to spark a direct confrontation. Royal has always taken it upon himself to police the boundaries of difference that separate the Tenenbaums from the rest, to define and enforce the limits of his collection, and in confronting the threat of Henry's usurpation he resorts to hatefully calling out the point of racial difference. Royal's racial provocations are one of a number of outlandishly inappropriate strategies of control that he employs, not least of which is pretending to be stricken with cancer; viewed from a distance, the audacity of these attempts is meant to be risible—as is the upper-crust myopic absurdity of evoking a musical and cultural icon like John Coltrane as a mark of derision. Royal's affront is, in one sense, just one of many instances of what MacDowell calls the "uncomfortable and painful humor" of Anderson's filmmaking, whose "preferred comic style is primarily a cold or detached one" (3). As several commentators have observed, it is a remarkable request that Anderson makes of his viewers here: to accept as the ostensible protagonist of his film a figure willing to engage in such racial baiting and to allow a measure of emotional recovery and reconciliation after Royal foregoes such taunts. As Rachel Dean-Ruzicka writes, "The problem herein lies not in the fact that Henry is a nice guy and Royal is not; it lies in the fact that Royal is the hero of the story. . . . Creating a hero from the white character (racist warts and all) undermines any power Henry's character might have had to destabilize white privilege in the film and family" (33). Royal's racist antagonism is clearly a strategy he is employing in defense of his collector's prerogative, for he easily abandons the stance and cheerfully works to enable the marriage of Etheline and Henry when he decides to forego his collector's privilege later in the film; yet the fact that Royal would think to employ such tactics at all evidences an unthinking comfort with his own racial privilege and a vast insensitivity to the histories and legacies of that privilege (to say nothing of its current political ramifications) that is deeply troubling—in regard to Royal himself, yes, but also in regard to Anderson's characterological choices. In Jonah Weiner's summation, "Anderson frequently points out his white characters' racial insensitivities . . . but he presents them, ultimately, as endearing quirks."

Exactly how endearing Royal's ugly racism is truly supposed to be is certainly open to question. Undoubtedly, it stands in the face of Anderson's own narrative and world-building proclivities, both in *Tenenbaums* itself and across his body of films. Anderson has often been accused of what Weiner calls a certain level of "unbearable whiteness," but his total filmic worlds are typically quite diverse. In contrast to certain predecessors and peers like Whit Stillman, Richard Linklater, Jason Reitman, or Alexander Payne, who often (though not always) choose to focus their films on a largely monoracial white social milieu, Anderson makes a point of casting his films in racial, ethnic, and religious shades evocative of their real-world referents: witness the mixture of Mexican American, Central American, and South Asian characters that populate the Dallas-inspired world of *Bottle Rocket*; the decidedly globalist crew of the *Belafonte* in *The Life Aquatic;* or the Hindus, Sikhs, and Catholics that populate *The Darjeeling Limited*'s Rajasthan. As Colleen Kennedy-Karpat has observed, "Anderson takes places that *could* be represented as culturally or ethnically narrow and carefully broadens them to emphasize diversity" (130; emphasis in original). In fact, four of Anderson's eight films climax in the marriage or romantic reunion of a mixed-race couple (a tally that might be one higher were the brief interracial affair in *The Darjeeling Limited* not so sordid and flagrantly self-destructive).[17] Yet Anderson's worlds almost inevitably *read* as white, which is largely a factor of what Hayot would call their "aesthetic amplitude," or "the relative spread of narrative attention across the diegesis" (56). As Hayot writes,

> Any work can mark some of its aspects as privileged by spending more time or space on them than on others, or by surrounding them with the privileged marks of aesthetic attention appropriate to the formal regime to which the work of art belongs: placing these aspects centrally in a frame, making them protagonists, allowing them to speak in direct or free indirect discourse, associating them with privileged paratexts (e.g. titles or epigraphs), and so on. (56)

With the singular exception of Zero in *The Grand Budapest Hotel*, Anderson's white characters are uniformly afforded greater aesthetic amplitude than any of their multiracial or multiethnic peers, quite literally occupying the central spaces of Anderson's narratives and frames. The irony here is that the most privileged positions in Anderson's filmic worlds are not necessarily the positions of greatest privilege: to a one, Anderson's protagonists are damaged, isolated, and deeply secretive or withdrawn. The amplitude of Anderson's filmic worlds aesthetically replicates this characterological myopia and solipsism, providing a distorted and nearly monoracial narrative view that stands in sharp contrast to the more diverse wider filmic context that Anderson also has constructed. In other words, there is typically a rich and diverse world all around Anderson's central characters, but it is one that they are almost always too self-absorbed to ever truly see. This is often but one symptom of those characters' wider pathologies, one more way that their worldview is revealed as destructive and distorted.

If Anderson's narrative strategy can be redeemed in the instance of Royal's racism, then, it is as a particularly acute manifestation of the larger pathology of Royal's general relationship with his family and with the world writ large, the self-appointed privilege he has claimed as collector rather than father—his overarching instinct to treat others as objects to be used to his own ends rather than as subjects to whom he owes any reciprocal responsibilities. Royal's proprietary stance is an ill that has long plagued the Tenenbaums, and it is only when that sickness borders on becoming terminal that he begins to rethink and to reform. That long-awaited reformation is triggered by the attempted suicide of Richie, which is ostensibly the result of his incestuous love for his sister Margot and his rage at learning of her many previous affairs yet which also is every bit the product of the troubled family-as-eclectic-collection structure of the Tenenbaum household. Royal has long guarded the boundaries of the family collection in particular by looking down on unapproved romantic relationships, as in his hurtful insistence on forgetting about Chas's wife even when he takes Chas and the grandchildren to the very cemetery where she is buried. Prior to her marriage to St. Clair, who seems to have a level of cultural prominence acceptable to the Tenenbaum clan, every single one of Margot's romantic relationships was conducted in secret. (Until it is discovered by a private detective later in the film, no one in the family ever even knew of her first marriage to the Jamaican reggae star.) Aside from the approved members of the Tenenbaum family, there simply seems to be almost no one deemed good enough. That Richie's first and strongest romantic attraction would be therefore turned inward within the members of this closed collective is perhaps only to be expected. Since their childhood together, Margot was always marked by their father as different by virtue of her adopted status yet still admissible in the Tenenbaum collection; Richie makes this very point when he confesses his love for Margot to Royal, claiming that his attraction to her is not technically incestuous by virtue of the adoption. Rather than expressing a psychological disturbance that is unique to him, Richie is merely enacting the logical conclusion of the pathological closedness that marks the Tenenbaums themselves. On some level, Royal realizes this. "I don't blame you, by the way," he says in response to Richie's confession of love. "She's a great looking girl, and she's smart as a whip." Which is to say, she's worthy of being a Tenenbaum.

Lest there be any doubt about Anderson's strident critique of this proprietary perspective, his cinematographic presentation of Richie and

Margot's relationship makes clear that it is both truly heartfelt *and* an impossible product of an emotionally distorted upbringing. For many commentators, the initial meeting of the adult Richie and the adult Margot at the port where Richie has disembarked from his travels is definitive to their relationship in the film, with Margot famously descending in slow motion from one of the ubiquitous Green Line buses to the strains of Nico's "These Days." Balanced equally in the centers of their respective frames, the two siblings and would-be lovers reduplicate one another in their point-of-view shot/reverse-shot meeting: They quite literally see themselves in one another. As always, Anderson's anamorphic widescreen aspect ratio produces a slight cylindrical distortion in these frames, and here Anderson chooses to deliberately emphasize the bending with prominent horizontal lines positioned in the diegetic visuals of each frame, the roofs of the buses on Margot's side and the port architecture on Richie's side cutting right above the heads of the two characters in their final shots of the sequence. The world is literally bending around them, changing its very shape in the face of their connection.

In the moment of the couple's near-consummation of that unspoken love later in the film, Anderson's frames makes no such accommodation. Surprising Margot inside the childhood tent he has established as his living space in the Tenenbaum living room, Richie initiates a series of jarringly mismatched shots between the two as they openly discuss their romantic feelings for the first time. Throughout the sequence, Richie is viewed in close-up only in frontal shots across the 180-degree line; Margot's close-ups all position her in profile at a 90-degree angle to the camera. Fixed together in a two-shot, the two characters can only face one another in a mismatched mirroring, Margot perched above Richie on the cot with her brother on the floor. They nearly align, but not quite. Willfully, Richie and Margot break through this misalignment in their one kiss in the film. Moving onto the cot, Richie brings himself into mirrored alignment with his sister at last, and it is from this position that they finally connect—all while a prominent seam in the tent wall behind them perfectly bifurcates the shot, literally drawing a line between the two Tenenbaums. Should there be any doubt about the nontranscendence of this kiss, Anderson has the two characters redouble their earlier cinematographic division in the very positioning of their bodies. Lying down together on the cot, Richie frontally faces the camera above while Margot rests on his chest, her face in profile once again. The idealistic mirroring of their first encounter at the port is rendered unrecoverable here. The sameness that they had been indoctrinated with as children and which they ultimately translated into an erotic ego-identification simply will not endure. For rock fans, Anderson embeds a subtle clue to this impossibility in the soundtrack of the scene, which emerges diegetically from a record that Margot plays inside the tent. That record is the Rolling Stones' *Between the Buttons*, and Romney marvels that "this may be the only film I have ever seen in which characters actually listen to two consecutive tracks from the same LP." The order of those tracks is all wrong, though: "She Smiled Sweetly" comes first in the film, followed by "Ruby Tuesday," while on the actual album the order is reversed and another song comes between. That song is "Connection"—the very element that is missed, both on the album and in the scene. Inside the collector's realm, any rearrangement and regrouping is possible. (Indeed, Richie's childhood car collection features prominently in the top right of the frame as he and Margot lie in one another's arms on the cot.) But that rearrangement cannot and will not translate outside the realm of the collection. The collection Royal made simply will not hold in the face of the world itself.

The issue, to incorporate the terms employed by Flatley, is one of sameness, difference, and similarity. Royal's Tenenbaum collection has long been marked by an aspiration not just to similarity but to sameness, much to its own detriment and disturbance. The members of the Tenenbaum clan have not just been Tenenbaums, they have been, to Royal at least, Royal Tenenbaums, iterations of his own being, all possessed of a fundamental kernel of identity beneath their different strengths and discordant eccentricities. This is the same pathological commitment to sameness manifested only somewhat more openly by Chas in his insistence that he and his sons wear identical tracksuits at all times. Of course, Chas's pathology results from his wife's sudden and tragic death. From what trauma this impulse originates for Royal himself, we cannot know, although his unusual obsession with his own mother's grave site—which he visits on two separate occasions in the film, treating the journey as a fun family outing—gives us some hint of his own unresolved sensations of loss. "Anybody feel like grabbing a couple of burgers and hitting the cemetery?" he asks cheerfully at one point.

Only when Royal, prompted by Richie's attempted suicide, endeavors to move beyond a stark dichotomy of identity and difference and at last allows the family to open itself to an ethos of similarity rather than sameness does the Tenenbaum's crisis begin to resolve. Citing his sudden realization that "I get it. He's everything I'm not," Royal unilaterally grants Etheline a divorce and hands her the requisite paperwork as Henry stands at her side. Royal undoubtedly overstates the case—Henry is not the destructive narcissist that Royal has proved himself to be, but the formerly wealthy New York litigator and the still wealthy New York accountant and property landlord have far more in common than Royal is perhaps willing to admit. (Royal in fact punctuates the encounter by complimenting Henry on the beautiful prewar apartment building he owns, likening it to his own uptown townhouse.) Though Royal has trouble moving beyond the poles of sameness and difference and mostly instead only shuttles between them, his two-decades-in-the-making relinquishing of his *ex-officio* role as head of the Tenenbaum household frees the other members of the family to rethink the boundaries of the collection of which they are all a part and to find a new logic of similarity by which to define themselves. Most important, Etheline formally accepts Henry's proposal, ushering in a new era in the Tenenbaum home, where the wedding will in fact take place. During the preparations, Chas realizes for the first time the similarity he shares with Henry, in that they are both widowers—a point that Henry, who was never blinded by the corrosive ideology of sameness underneath the Tenenbaum identity, of course knew all along. And although Richie claims to remain in love with Margot, their circumstances no longer seem as dire or desperate as they did at the time of his suicide attempt: "I think we're just going to have to be secretly in love with each other and leave it at that, Richie," she tells him at the end of their scene together—and promptly leaves the tent and the collected world that it encapsulates. By the end of the film, she has finally returned to writing plays. A new world has opened up beyond the rigid boundaries of the Tenenbaum name that had for so long defined them both.

It is in large part because of this joyous reformation of the collective Tenenbaum identity that Anderson is able to pull off the remarkable feat of ending his film with an exuberant depiction of the funeral of his main character, offering the burial service as a ceremony that is neither solemn nor cynical. To the upbeat strains of Van Morrison's "Everyone," the immediate and affiliate members of the Tenenbaum clan lay Royal to rest in the cemetery he had visited so many times during his life. His burial is a marker of their liberation from the limited and limiting notions of collective identity that he imposed and that they for so long accepted. But it also is a marker of Royal's own liberation from his past misdeeds and the rewriting of a legacy that could have been much darker. The one bequest the impoverished Royal is able to leave his family—that set of Encyclopedia Britannica about which he always was so concerned—is both pathetic for a man of his former wealth and perfectly fitting for the new world he has handed over for them to make. Benjamin writes that every true collection constitutes for its collector "a whole magic encyclopedia, a world order" (*Arcades* 207). Royal has left to his family the world itself, everything from A to Z, newly expansive and free of his mark.

The Darjeeling Limited (2007)   Against the somewhat paradoxical exuberance of *Tenenbaums'* funeral ending stands the much darker thematics of *The Darjeeling Limited*, which is in many ways *Tenenbaums'* more cynical companion film. Released six years after *Tenenbaums*, with *The Life Aquatic* coming between, *Darjeeling* is Anderson's next film to explicitly consider a family in turmoil and attempting to reform itself, returning to many of the tropes and themes of *Tenenbaums* but beginning with an opposite set of premises. If *Tenenbaums* is the story of adult siblings who retreat to their childhood homestead and must navigate the demands and limitations imposed by an overly controlling father figure who pushes his way back into their life, *Darjeeling* follows a set of adult siblings who escape to a wholly temporary and transitory space on the opposite side of the world from which they grew up, searching for a mother who abandoned them long ago and has no interest in reconnecting. Both are stories of families coming together again for the first time in the wake of a recent and unexpected death and haunted by a cleaving apart by separation or divorce decades ago. Both concern the delicate processes by which such families must calibrate the degree of their closedness and openness to the world, the extent to which they represent a special collection of unique individuals set apart from the world—the *royal* Tenenbaums—and the extent to which they are just a group of people thrown together by genetic lottery and happy to be rid of one another as soon as possible. If *Tenenbaums* is a story of a family unit whose bonds are wound far too tight, *Darjeeling* is the examination of a family whose bonds are so loose they run the risk of slipping away entirely. "I wonder if the three of us would have been friends in real life. Not as brothers, but as people," Jack asks his brothers not long before they are scheduled to depart for flights to different corners of the globe. "We might've had a better chance, I guess," his brother Peter replies. Here family runs the risk not of being a mechanism for the enforcement of sameness but a means by which difference might be most painfully exposed, giving the lie to the idea of any possible collective identity in this world and instead presenting as truth the idea that the dispersion the collector always seeks so desperately to avoid is in fact inevitable.

Like *Tenenbaums*, then, *Darjeeling* must be regarded as a meditation on loss, another film specifically set in the wake of great trauma whose actions unfold in response to events that predate the start of the film's diegetic chronology. The father of the Whitman clan, a man about whom we know very little beyond the fact that he was a figure of some wealth, died a year before the start of the film's action. The Whitman boys' mother was living abroad at the time and chose not to come back for the funeral; we are led to presume the parents had been separated or divorced for many years. The mother has not been heard from since declining to pay her former husband any final respects. It is this fraught back story, which hangs over the events of the film like a storm cloud, that can at least to some degree help contextualize what many critics have found to be the film's most problematic aspects—namely, its notably minimal engagement with any actual specifics of the Indian cultures it uses as its visual backdrops, what Weiner calls "an entire race and culture . . . turned into therapeutic scenery." Francis (Owen Wilson), Jack (Jason Schwartzman), and Peter (Adrien Brody)—the heroes of Anderson's epic journey across the backcountry of Rajasthan—claim to show an interest in the country and culture to which the search for their mother has brought them, yet their actual interaction with the world around them for the most part adds up to little more than buying various souvenirs and volunteering such idiotic sentiments as "I love the way this country smells. I'll never forget it. It's kind of spicy." Among the array of characters who populate Anderson's films, there is no shortage of narcissistic and self-involved individuals, but even by these standards the Whitman brothers may be among the most pathologically myopic. In Anderson's own characterization of the brothers in a later interview, "They're kind of interested. They like the idea of picking up a little of this and a little of that, but they're not really studying it for long. They'll just put it in their suitcase with the rest of their stuff. . . . They're just very selfish, narcissistic people" (qtd. in Seitz 209). The problem, writes Browning, is that this diegetic myopia seems to extend to a general myopia in the film's construction as well: "It tells us virtually nothing of the country but only of the narcissistic cultural obsessions of some of those passing through it" (87).

But like so many of Anderson's films, *Darjeeling* takes place in a state of emotional retreat for its main characters, and this context is important for approaching the relationship of traveler and host culture depicted in the film. Unlike the Tenenbaum children, the Whitmans have no nostalgic structure of their own to which they can retire and inside of which they can barricade themselves amid tents and bunk beds. (As far as we know within the film, there is no family real estate at all anymore—the characters make no mention of any, though there is certainly no shortage of remaining wealth.) Instead, the Whitman boys are attempting a retreat to the body of their mother herself: literally seeking out her person as a way of responding to the traumatic loss of their father, a man with whom she herself no longer wanted any association. Theirs is an almost primal search for origins set in the face of an archetypal loss of authority and order. Against a mother who has refused to collect them—in the literal sense of coming to fetch them and in the figurative sense of providing them some sense of order and identity in the wake of their family's loss—they have come with an entreaty to be collected. In this sense, the film enacts an ironic reversal of the standard trope by which the Westerner comes to India for purposes of collection and expropriation, be it spiritual or material. As Peter Hoffenberg has observed of the subcontinent's relationship to Anglo-European practices of collection and display at the height of the British Empire in the nineteenth century, the public exhibition of artifacts from India offered "spectacles of tangible fantasy," vesting the British public with "the power to organize, study, and compare" as a means of asserting and enacting cultural superiority (xv). Needless to say, Anderson's latter-day travelers exhibit no such impulses toward callous expropriation and intercultural negotiation; to the contrary, they can hardly be bothered to notice the world around them much at all. The degree to which the Whitman brothers prove hopelessly unable to grapple in any meaningful way with a culture as visually arresting and spiritually capacious as that of Rajasthan is itself a yardstick against which we may judge the depths of their posttraumatic alienation and emotional retreat, the degree to which they have each shrunk into themselves. Those commentators, like Dean-Ruzicka, who have struggled with what they feel is the appropriation of the film's Indian setting in the service of "a generic spiritual awakening" (36) may in fact be significantly overestimating the degree to which the Whitman brothers learn much of anything at all on their ultimately failed journey. There is a show of emotional growth that the boys make toward each other near the end of the film, but Anderson gives us almost no reason to believe any of it and provides significant indications that we should not. *Darjeeling* is arguably one of the director's darkest films, a study in what it means to be alone and closed to the world, unable to find any group in which one might belong.

The first signs of this trauma begin, importantly, in *Darjeeling*'s prequel short *Hotel Chevalier*, which was screened alongside *The Darjeeling Limited* at the film's premiere and then released on Apple iTunes. A brief and largely plotless tale of Jack's experiences in a hotel room in Paris before leaving to meet his brothers in India, the film stages in its *mise-en-scène* the traumatic state in which each of the brothers is in some way living. Jack has been existing in this stately but modestly sized suite for an unknown duration—"more than a month," he admits to the unnamed ex-girlfriend who visits him, and it is unclear whether he actually knows the full amount of time beyond that. When we first see Jack, he is visually presented as being dead: his feet and partially robed legs poking out of the far right side of the frame in a doubling of the physical position of the dead bodies covered by blankets in the Billy Wilder film he is watching on television, *Stalag 17* (fig. 12). Of course, Jack is physically alive, but just how much so remains in question. Around the temporary space of the hotel room he has laid out the items of an eccentric personal collection of expensive tchotchkes and high-end bric-a-brac: a small porcelain statute of Winston Churchill, a set of three wind-up music boxes, a pinned butterfly and dragonfly in a shadow box. Jack is living inside a kind of literal manifestation of Benjamin's description of the collection as the "phantasmagoria of the interior" (*Arcades* 14), having responded to his father's death by retreating into a temporary and largely anonymous space onto which he has imposed whatever tokens of his interiority he can bring with him. It is a strange conceit, bringing along one's pinned insects to place in one's hotel room abroad—and Jack's ex-girlfriend (Natalie Portman) points it out as such, handling the shadow box at one point and looking at him quizzically (fig. 13). Jack is literally the collector in retreat, hiding from the world and surrounded by his collection, stuck within his own self-

Figure 12. Jack in repose |

Figure 13. Regarding Jack's phantasmagoria of
the interior |

projection. As his ex-girlfriend surveys the hotel room, Peter Sarstedt's "Where Do You Go To (My Lovely)" plays on the soundtrack, with the singer crooning "Tell me the thoughts that surround you. I want to look inside your head." Indeed, perhaps the only relationship that Jack truly has left is with his things. When we first see his full body on the hotel bed, he is framed in an off-center single shot where various items from his collection—a few books, a CD—lie next to him on the other side of the king-sized bed, taking up the symmetrical space where a romantic partner should lie. Jack does have a romantic liaison of sorts, but his paramour never takes up this position of equal partnership on his bed. She is not girlfriend but ex-girlfriend, and there is no thought of a renewed long-term relationship; she pushed to be let up to his room for the night because they were both in Paris, and he reluctantly consented. In the absence of anything else to do, she and Jack are happy enough to continue indulging what lust remains between the two of them long after they have given up on love. The most commitment she can muster is to say "Whatever happens in the end, I don't want to lose you as my friend," to which Jack responds "I promise, I will never be your friend." Absent any real family structure and without a romantic partner or any friends to speak of, Jack seems about as lonely in his room in the Hotel Chevalier as one can be in a luxury hotel, which seems to be quite lonely indeed. For whose benefit the spreading of his collected objects around the room is intended is unclear if not for his own, a reminder to himself that he still exists and that he has an interior life of some kind even if it feels like he does not.

This is the context of Jack's trip to India, and in fact it is the most benign back story of the three brothers. Peter, we learn slowly over the course of the film, has come on this journey to India even though his wife is due to give birth to their first child in a matter of weeks, and for reasons that are never made explicitly clear he has neither told her where he was going or why nor told his brothers before about the child he is soon expecting. Francis, for his part, arrives in India with his face covered in elaborate bandages like some victim of a cartoon explosion. He claims to be recovering from a car crash but later reveals that the wounds are from a suicide attempt. It was in the wake of this secondary trauma stemming from their father's death months before that he first hatched the idea of traveling to India with Jack and Peter, planning the journey with the meticulous attention to structure and willful disregard for contingency of Dignan from *Bottle Rocket*. (He even has his assistant bring along a laminating machine to use on board the train when printing their daily schedules, a potent metaphor for the brothers' own vacuum-sealed relationship to the world around them.) Still recovering from his brush with mortality, Francis attempts to be the authority figure and pillar of organization that he most needs and that he assumes his brothers do as well—collecting them together, providing them with a daily set of spelled out edicts and directions, even ordering for them at mealtime (a habit, we learn, he has picked up from their absentee mother). If, in the wake of their father's death and their mother's abandonment, the Whitman brothers are left without the structure and order that family provides even into adulthood, Francis is determined to will those aspects into being—if only because he himself needs them desperately. If no one in the world particularly cares what becomes of the Whitman brothers, he will be their collector, putting on a show of playing the kind of figure that came so naturally to Royal. Francis even goes so far as to try to expropriate his brothers' passports in the name of safe keeping, a more legalistic and material manifestation of Royal's attempt to collect and own the identities of the Tenenbaum clan.

The goal, Francis says, is for the brothers to reconnect and learn an important lesson in spirituality. "I want us to be completely open and say yes to everything—even if it's shocking and painful," he says, in no way appreciating the degree to which his damaged and disheveled brothers are not up to the severe emotional demands of this task. Their very first evening in country is spent trading back and forth prescription medications they were able to purchase off the shelf in Indian pharmacies before getting on the train, drugging themselves into a suitable stupor. Throw in a torrid seduction scene with an unhappy stewardess on the train—essentially Jack's idea of working through his mixed emotions about sleeping with his ex—and you have a night in which the depressed and semisuicidal Whitman brothers have said yes to nothing except drugs and sex, hardly an auspicious start to their spiritual reawakening.

Such is the nature of the brothers' journey toward the mountains where their mother is hiding from them. Presented with a countryside and social landscape as physically and culturally rich as any they could visit, they remain entirely imprisoned by concerns that wholly predate their arrival in this place, sometimes quite literally so. A stop at the bazaar in Jodhpur turns into an attempt to secure a working power adapter that they forgot to bring with them; a visit to a religious temple turns into a fight about passports and a spat over an expensive belt. In the absence of any greater purpose, the brothers succumb to a drive toward acquisition that doesn't even rise to the level of collection. Francis buys one shoe to replace a loafer that was stolen by a shoeshine boy, not even deigning to buy a full pair. For no particular reason whatsoever except perhaps the fulfillment of Orientalist fantasies mixed with a not-so-latent death wish, Peter makes the mystifying decision to purchase a venomous cobra, which he attempts to keep in a cardboard box in their train compartment. Francis's laminated cards notwithstanding, the boys' spiritual journey is a material and spiritual shambles, an unholy jumble of self-destructive impulses, petty rivalries, and short attention spans. It should tell you something when a director as meticulous about symmetry as Anderson sees fit to represent the three brothers shoved together in their train car in any number of surprising and asymmetrical visual combinations, bodies askew and heads hanging upside down off of bunk beds (fig. 14). To an extent far beyond that which they care to acknowledge or to recognize, the boys are on a train to nowhere—a point made literal when they are angrily booted from the sleeper in a rural village for bringing the cobra on board and are forced to spend the night alone in the wilderness.

This is the point at which everything is supposed to change for the brothers, and much of how one reacts to the film depends on the impres-

Figure 14. Asymmetrical framing aboard the
Darjeeling Limited

sion that one takes from the events that transpire after that literal night in the wilderness, when the brothers attempt to save three young boys who have been swept up by the current while trying to ford a river. In a much-cited review of the film, Weiner argues that the funeral sequences that follow for the one boy the brothers could not save are a tired recapitulation of Westerner-as-savior tropes. "This isn't just heavy-handed, it's offensive. In a grisly little bit of developing-world outsourcing, the child does the bothersome work of dying so that the American heroes won't have to die spiritually." Yet the dark irony of these sequences lies in the very degree to which they have no real impact on the brothers at all. These three brothers—who together are so alone either by circumstance or willful choice that almost no one in the world knows or particularly cares where they are right now and who are so distraught by the events of their own lives that one of them seems on the verge of abandoning his soon-to-be-born child—by chance find themselves in the midst of a tight-knit village bound by ties of kinship and culture whose inhabitants have invited them to partake in a profound ritual of mourning that they really have no business attending, and yet they neither observe nor learn anything of substance.

In fact, Anderson's depiction of the brothers' journey to the funeral is deliberately evocative of the train ride itself. Scored to "Strangers" by The Kinks, the lead-up to the funeral ceremony speaks of an emotional and spiritual journey born of spiritual sharing and material release:

> 'Till peace we find tell you what I'll do
> All the things I own I will share with you
> If I feel tomorrow like I feel today
> We'll take what we want and give the rest away
> Strangers on this road we are on
> We are not two we are one.

But the scene that unfolds beneath these words belies such attempts at connection and understanding. Emerging from the hut they were given to prepare themselves for the rites, all three bedecked in flowing traditional garments, the brothers walk in slow motion to the vehicle that will carry them to the ceremony, parked across the village. All around them, elaborate preparations are being made, but the boys travel an improbably straight and uninterrupted line through this visual cacophony; even more improbably, all the manifold preparations align themselves neatly into the foreground and background planes, leaving the middle plane completely open across the full tracking shot. Like travelers bound to an unstoppable vehicle—that is, like passengers on a train—the three Whitmans gaze around them in wonderment at the village but never stop moving, looking at the villagers as if peering through invisible windows as they pass right by them. Their motion is entirely unbroken, their relationship to the passing world arranged perfectly on either side of them entirely encased and passive. The double irony here is that the camera capturing the brothers' trainlike procession through the village is itself structurally evocative of their greater train ride through the country, Anderson's unbroken tracking shot accomplished by literally laying tracks across the village landscape and moving the camera on a dolly. Here that camera movement fills in for and reminds us of the invisible force of locomotion still propelling the brothers past any true human connections and past any appreciation beyond the merely touristic. In truth, the boys have never gotten off the train that brought them to this place; they bring it with them wherever they go. Their relationship to the world around them is so thoroughly laminated that they do not even think to ask for anyone's names, let alone for an explanation of what is happening before them or in what way they should properly participate. They are content merely to gawk at the whole affair from behind glass, even as they stand in its very midst.

Which is not to say they are engaged in any kind of forward motion. To the contrary, during their trip to the funerary rites they are brought back vividly to an incident before their own father's funeral, directly shown in flashback, in which they failed to rescue his Porsche from an auto repair shop with the aim of driving it to his funeral but did succeed in finding the last item in his collection of eleven monogramed Luis Vuitton suitcases, which they are now somewhat morbidly dragging around with them on their journey. Surrounded in the Indian village by a real instance of deeply meaningful ritual action, the kind of experience they have been searching for all along, all the brothers can think back to are *things*, the high-end collector's items in which they have stored away their emotions. They cannot even recognize the very communality and collectivity that they each so desperately desire when it is presented to them, not even enough to naïvely romanticize it. There is no noticeable change in the brothers' behavior after the supposedly transformative experience of the funeral. They petulantly decide to abandon the search for their mother, then impulsively decide to continue it at the last moment. Peter has a horrendous argument with his horrified wife over an airport telephone line (learning incidentally that she has had a sonogram and he is going to have a son), only to then decide to stay in the country even longer rather than return to her. They surreptitiously fill their sweet drinks with alcohol from a flask lest they confront the world uninebriated, and they continue on their way. The kind of spiritual peace and sense of cosmological order for which the brothers claim to be searching cannot be had on the cheap, nor can it simply be borrowed from other cultures, and no rural funeral ceremony can change that.

Nor apparently does the devoted and disciplined search for that order necessarily yield much in the way of human compassion, to say nothing of motherly love. When the brothers eventually do make it to their mother, they find her in a Catholic convent surrounded by children whom she serves, none of them her own. Patricia's (Anjelica Huston) response to the appearance of her boys, whom she had tried to dissuade from coming in a letter warning them of a man-eating tiger in the area, is essentially to perform a kind of long-form confidence game, quieting their anxieties and concerns with a long list of emotional tasks they will tackle the next day when they are all properly rested and then taking their orders for breakfast before urging them to sleep, only to use the cover of night to steal away and disappear on them again. (She does leave breakfast.) In her place within the carefully ordered and hierarchical structures of the Catholic Church, Sister Patricia has in a way found the kind of community and collectivity for which so many Anderson characters search, albeit with a more overtly religious bent than most. Yet there is clearly no place in that collectivity for her own children, whom she must keep excised and whom she can barely stand to see. In contrast to Etheline Tenenbaum, who allowed her children to return to the family home on even the flimsiest of pretenses, and even in contrast to Royal Tenenbaum, who tried desperately to join his children there whether they wanted him or not, Patricia makes it clear to her sons that there is no family for them anymore beyond whatever family structure they can cobble together themselves. The boys' response to their mother's disappearance is to attempt to cover over the event with a bizarre religious ritual of their own creation, one they have been trying to get right at different points throughout their journey. They claim to themselves to have at last performed it correctly, though by what standard is hard to tell: The ceremony is mostly a combination of faux Tai Chi and half-baked shamanism, performed in a country with religious traditions that go back millennia. Mostly they seem to be haphazardly physicalizing their own emotional pain and calling it release.

For many commentators, the ending of *Darjeeling* represents a kind of unearned emotional success. For the Whitman brothers, Barry Stephenson writes, "a rhythm beyond their own making takes charge, and they must yield and follow the course of events that unfold. No longer do they try to create a container in which their experience can be distilled and repackaged; rather, they are contained and carried." Such terms of emotional transcendence certainly capture how the brothers might like to see the journey themselves. Anderson allows the three men to finally achieve a kind of even balance in their framing, positioning them in a triangle in the frame as their mountaintop religious ceremony concludes—a rather intuitive blocking arrangement that has been used infrequently in the film and implies a level of physical and emotional calm that they have at last achieved. This implication is redoubled when the boys are forced at last to discard all the luggage they have been dragging through the subcontinent in order to make it onto their departing train. Baggage left literally behind, Jack and Peter make a show of allowing Francis to finally hold onto their passports for them, consenting to the collection effort and the internal hierarchy he has been trying to impose since the beginning. And yet, any action so literal and clichéd as the discarding of baggage (and baggage that was actually inherited from their father, no less) should be viewed with a certain amount of skepticism. For all its mildly celebratory aspects, the end of *Darjeeling* also has a deliberately recursive quality that works against the narrative of progress and change: The brothers go through the same actions in the opening moments on their new train as they did on their old train—presenting their tickets, accepting a sweet lime drink—only more cheerfully and without spiking the drinks with alcohol. If this is progress, it is baby steps only. More to the point is the insert that Anderson includes shortly before this final train ride, one of his classic dollhouse-style pans across an imagined train containing compartments representing the experiences of many of the minor characters from across the film: Jack's ex-girlfriend is pictured alone in a hotel room, Francis's disgruntled assistant is on a plane ride back to the United States, the stewardess with whom Jack had his brief affair is pictured smoking alone, the unnamed American businessman shown racing for a train in the movie's opening moments is here seated and relaxed at last, a pregnant woman who is presumably Peter's wife sits alone on a bed, even the man-eating tiger of Patricia's description is given a jungle-strewn compartment on the train. All the characters are alone and isolated, the same state to which the three Whitman brothers are about to return as they go their separate ways.

Anderson's brief forays into the narrative afterlives of minor characters who departed the film at various earlier points calls us to wonder what will become of the Whitman boys themselves after their experiment in familial reformation has been completed and their own narrative line is officially done, and from this perspective Anderson's decision to end the soundtrack of the film with Joe Dassin's "Aux Champs-Élysées" is an ominous choice. Directly recalling Jack's experiences in the *Hotel Chevalier* prequel, the buoyant music cue calls up memories of his emotional isolation and figurative deadness. He claims to his brothers that he will not be going to Italy to meet up with his ex-girlfriend as she had requested, but where else will he go that will offer him anything other than another luxurious and lonely retreat? And if Jack's story is as cyclical as the music implies, what of the other brothers? What guarantee do we have that Peter actually plans to go home to his wife and child at all and will not simply disappear on them for good the way his mother did to him? What is to say that Francis with his brothers now gone will not attempt suicide again, especially since the grand plan to bring mother and children back together, hatched in the wake of his last suicide, has objectively failed? These questions lay embedded in the final moments of Anderson's film, but unlike *Tenenbaums*, *Darjeeling* offers no promises of a renewed and revitalized family or a renewed and revitalized community. The absence of community is isolation, and the absence of the collection is dispersion. One shudders to think of the destination to which this train is headed.

***Fantastic Mr. Fox* (2009)**   Of Anderson's three films that deal explicitly with families, *Fantastic Mr. Fox* is by far the most positive. Released two years after *The Darjeeling Limited*, the film contains none of the darker familial themes the director dealt with in that earlier work—at least, that is, not directly on its meticulously designed surface. *Fantastic Mr. Fox* does in fact tacitly acknowledge much of the same material about familial dissolution and the difficulty of negotiating familial identity that pervades films like *The Royal Tenenbaums* and *The Darjeeling Limited*; the difference is that in this film, for once, the greater consequences of these issues are effectively forestalled before they have a chance to manifest themselves. The issues of familial breakdown that haunt those earlier films never quite materialize, though they are always lurking at the margins: indeed, those issues do in fact come remarkably close to appearing full force at points. Multiple times throughout the story, separation or divorce are hinted at as possible outcomes of Mr. Fox's (George Clooney) selfish behavior, leading one to imagine an alternate animated universe where the Fox family has not remained so close-knit. "If what I think is happening *is* happening, it better not be," Felicity Fox (Meryl Streep) threatens at one point, "ominously" according to the script. Or, even more pointedly, "I love you too, but I shouldn't have married you," she says. What is perhaps most remarkable about sentiments such as these within the film is that they are not hyperbolic tropes of familial strain that can be easily overcome; rather, they are severe but emotionally appropriate responses to what are some rather serious character shortcomings on the part of the supposedly fantastic Mr. Fox. Perhaps alone among animated characters in widely released Hollywood films, Mr. Fox is a figure who takes his loving family for granted and willfully acts against their safety and security for no other reason than his own self-gratification, to say nothing of his haughty disregard for the wider animal community of which his family is a part. "I have this thing," he openly admits, "where I need everybody to think I'm the greatest— the quote-unquote fantastic Mr. Fox—and if they aren't completely knocked-out, dazzled, and kind of intimidated by me, then I don't feel good about myself." (There is a subtle parallel here to the secretive and partially self-serving father in Brad Bird's Pixar feature *The Incredibles*, though at least Mr. Incredible had the not insignificant excuse of trying to save the world through his surreptitious actions rather than simply stealing a couple of chickens.) A sort of spiritual animal cousin to Royal Tenenbaum, Mr. Fox starts the film with the kind of contented family life and placid collective community for which so many Anderson characters actively pine, only to come within a hair's breadth of wantonly throwing them both away by film's end. He does not in fact do so, of course, and there is no traumatizing scene of animated animals getting divorced to mar the family-friendly surface of this fable. But Mr. Fox's actions are not without larger consequences—consequences that are not just visited on himself but on the whole animal collective that has kept him as a member. In this way, *Fantastic Mr. Fox* comes closer than one might imagine a PG-rated animated film ever could to aligning to the darker themes of Anderson's filmmaking. It is a fable to be sure, but one uniquely in keeping with the wider Anderson universe.

This element of the film's simultaneous connection to and departure from Anderson's standard filmmaking universe in terms of its narrative and thematics holds for the picture's visual construction as well. As the only animated entry in Anderson's filmography so far, *Fantastic Mr. Fox* is both a kind of apotheosis of Anderson's established visual world and a substantial change from certain aspects of his live-action filmmaking. As a manifestation of Anderson's *mise-en-scène*, the film offers a kind of explosion of the director's typical visual universe: complete with animal characters marked equally by the actual animal fur painstakingly stitched onto each figure (which the animators had to carefully blow on between takes to simulate its natural movements) and by the tiny bespoke clothing meticulously crafted for each character, the film approaches the level of pure style exercise, a kind of fever-dream of Andersonisms in which the homespun, taxidermied art direction for which he has become famous has suddenly come vividly to life on its own without any intervening need for flesh-and-blood actors or real-world sets. As Browning writes, "*Fantastic Mr. Fox* provides Anderson with elements ideal for his filmmaking aesthetic: a fictional world entirely at his disposal, which he can control to a greater extent than any of his previous work, and the possibility to indulge fully his penchant for characters who are quirky yet engaging and pack the frame with detail so that it not only rewards repeat viewing on DVD, it almost demands it" (89). Liberated from the practical and logistical (not to mention gravitational) demands of live-action shooting, Anderson's visual constructions are here for the first time free to iterate and expand into ever more elaborate versions of his typical imagery and structures. Hence the elaborate underground warrens created by the fleeing animals by film's end and shown in detail by Anderson in glorious, intricate cross-sections that make the train cross-section from *Darjeeling* seem like child's play, replaced here by something approaching an elaborate ant farm crafted almost entirely at right angles. Or the map that Felicity draws of the whole animated universe of the film, which begins as a practical exercise for planning purposes akin to the diegetic drawings of many other Anderson characters and then expands into what is effectively a (miniature) Diego Rivera–sized mural of the total Fox universe and also an elaborate metastylistic exercise, an actual painting of an animated universe rendered inside the actual miniature version of that same universe. At the same time, *Fox*'s status as an animated fable lends a kind of literalness to much of what was left implicit in Anderson's other films, giving this work at times a downright nightmarish fairy-tale quality not found elsewhere in his canon. Although the characters in films like *Tenenbaums* and *Darjeeling* might worry about the corrosive forces of loneliness, disappointment, and dispersion that beset them in maturity, the danger faced by the Fox family threatens to actually tear apart their world in a much more literal way. It is a series of three apocalyptic bulldozers, not abstract anxieties, that come to destroy the Fox family and literally demolish the place where they live. Likewise the desperate and all-too-literal retreat into ever deeper layers of seclusion and isolation as the animals tunnel further and further below ground to escape such terrible forces, enacting physically what many of Anderson's characters—the brothers of *The Darjeeling Limited* foremost among them—have experienced emotionally.

Of course, not all these elements belong entirely or only to Anderson's filmic world, *Fantastic Mr. Fox* being to date his only direct (or semidirect) adaptation of another author's work. So much of the story is new to Anderson's version of it—from Ash's mission to rescue his father's tail to the commentaries of the television crew—that the word *adaptation* doesn't seem to quite convey the relationship of filmmaker and source, which was more a kind of creative collaboration or a co-imagination with a preexisting literary work. Anderson and his film's marketers essentially admitted as much in the unique way in which they promoted the picture, putting Anderson together with Roald Dahl's widow Felicity in public interviews to discuss how, in Felicity's words, "Wes has expanded [the story] in the true spirit of the book, and of

Roald particularly" (Specter). Anderson's fidelity to the literal version of Dahl's original text never really claimed to go much past basic inspiration and broad outline, and as if by way of compensation for his narrative departures, he made a deliberate point of visually adapting Dahl's world itself. Hence the somewhat unusual choice made by Anderson and his animators to recreate in miniature aspects of Dahl's house in the diegetic world of the film. Most of the elements of furniture and set dressing in the film were painstakingly recreated from Gipsy House, Dahl's home in Buckinghamshire, and Anderson's rendering of the above-ground world of the film held a similar relationship to Dahl's visual universe, both lived and imagined. The English countryside town in which much of the above-ground action unfolds in the latter half of the film is based on Dahl's own home town of Great Missenden, and aspects of the production design—including the look of Mr. Fox himself—are indebted to the illustrations of Donald Chaffin from Knopf's U.S. first edition of the book. Dahl even appears in the film in a way, the character of Franklin Bean being visually based on his stature and visage—Adrienne Kertzer calls him a "scary version of Roald Dahl" (7) (fig. 15). (Surely there is an intentionally ironic resonance in Bean's desire in the film to catch and to literally curtail Mr. Fox, who has far exceeded the narrative boundaries of Dahl's original story in much the same way as he smuggles himself across Bean's established farm boundaries in the film.) Anderson's collector's impulse is at work again, taking assorted bits and pieces of Dahliana—a

Figure 15. A very scary version of Roald Dahl

furnishing here, a storybook illustration there—and recombining them into an ostensible tribute to Dahl that bears every hallmark of being a Wes Anderson composite.

And nowhere is Anderson's collector's impulse more at work than in the narrative of the film, which takes the basic signposts of Dahl's story and overlays them with the primary concerns of the Andersonian filmic universe, the questions of collecting and collectivity that pervade all his works. Hence, at the film's center, the potentially destructive and undoubtedly selfish actions of Anderson's version of Dahl's vulpine *pater familias*, who is guilty of many of the same actions that have caused so much hurt when performed by other parents or parental figures in Anderson's films. First and foremost is Mr. Fox's decision to move his family out of their less-than-glamorous hole in the ground into a more upscale home in an above-ground tree, a move ostensibly undertaken for the benefit of all that was in fact designed to narrowly serve the interests of Mr. Fox himself even at the price of putting those he supposedly loves in mortal danger, given that the tree was in full view of the Boggis, Bunce, and Bean farms from which Mr. Fox intended to steal. This very brand of selfishness disguised as either generosity or practicality was a specialty of Royal Tenenbaum's reckless daredevilry and a frequent undertaking of Steve Zissou, who almost never failed to put his film and budget above the safety of his cast and crew. Likewise Mr. Fox's undisguised favoritism toward his nephew Kristofferson (Eric Anderson) at the emotional expense of his own son Ash (Jason Schwartzman), a replay of the game of favorites Royal played among his own children and that seemed to mark the brief relationship between Patricia and her three boys seen in *The Darjeeling Limited*. Ash is clearly hurt by the lack of attention from his father, but Mr. Fox never seems to care and goes right on devaluing his son's abilities, even at the very moment the boy most needs encouragement. "I never would've involved your cousin if I realized you would feel this way. It was only ever just because he's kind of a natural," Mr. Fox says by way of a half-hearted apology at one point. Then there is the not insignificant matter of Mr. Fox's broken pledge, a flagrant violation of the agreement he made to his wife "to find another line of work" after they had children, flaunted for no better reason than the fact that he thinks he can somehow get away with it now. "I'm a wild animal. . . . I'm trying to tell you the truth about myself," he says by way of an explanation for his actions at one point, vocalizing a sentiment that would sound equally plausible coming out of the mouth of Royal Tenenbaum. He has needs too, the safety of his family and friends be damned.

Of course, this being an animated tale, the ramifications of Mr. Fox's indulgence in his most self-serving instincts is not so much an emotional catastrophe for those around him as a literal one. No grand machines of violence attacked the Tenenbaum children after Royal held his disastrous parental meeting about his impending separation from Etheline, and no actual enemies bent on killing and skinning anyone they could find pursued the Whitman brothers when their mother entirely forsook them for her religious calling. But these are the consequences that Mr. Fox's child, wife, and nephew—and eventually his neighbors as well—must all confront as a result of his exercises in self-actualization. The landscape of wreckage and destruction left by farmers Boggis, Bunce, and Bean in the aftermath of their animal pursuit is a potent visual metaphor for the emotional devastation that haunts the places and people of Anderson's live-action films. Where once there was a loving family home and with it a sense of structure and ordered domesticity, there is now just a giant gaping crater (fig. 16). But it is not just a trail of general physical destruction that follows Mr. Fox's action; there is an equal degree of collateral damage inflicted directly on those for whom he cares. Seeking to win some measure of approval from his father, Ash conspires with Kristofferson to try to steal back the tail that was so humiliatingly shot off of Mr. Fox during one of his break-ins at the farms. Yet Ash's well-intentioned but ultimately misguided attempt to attend to and salve his father's wounds, emotional and physical, only ends up endangering everyone further, leading to Kristofferson's capture and imprisonment; the train of consequences stemming from Mr. Fox's briefly unbridled selfishness leads to a world in which no one around Mr. Fox is safe anymore, even those he most favored. One can see very easily why Felicity would reproach her husband in the most extreme of ways, telling him that "in the end, we all die—unless you change." He has very nearly destroyed their entire known physical world and put in danger everyone in it.

Mr. Fox's salvation—a unique narrative element in *Fantastic Mr. Fox* among Anderson's family-focused films—is the willingness of the larger

Figure 16. Emotional and physical wreckage in
Fantastic Mr. Fox

animal community to close ranks around the Fox family and work together with them in their escape from trouble, even though that trouble, which affects them all, was of Mr. Fox's own misguided making. As a family, the Foxes have what none of the other Anderson filmic families could ever dream of finding: a community that extends beyond the small family unit and that accepts the Fox family members as its own not on the basis of exact identity but on the grounds of similarity. In other words, a collective, per Flatley's usage of the term as a group defining itself by likeness. *Fantastic Mr. Fox* is perhaps the Anderson film that is least interested diegetically in issues of collecting—the animals worry more about the prospect of *being* collected and added to a taxidermy display (a not unreasonable fear in view of Anderson's own past production design, particularly in *The Royal Tenenbaums*) than of maintaining any collections of their own. But it is perhaps correspondingly the Anderson film most explicitly interested in issues of actual collectivity and the ways in which groups beyond the family and beyond the tenuous constructions of individuals seeking to will a community into existence can function. There is no shortage of animus toward Mr. Fox for the pain and destruction his actions have wrought, yet there is no suggestion within the animal community that they are not all in this together. "We don't like you, and we hate your dad," one of the animals says to Ash in the midst of the crisis, but they remain together as a group trying to dig their way to safety. It is one thing for the Fox family to stick together: their fundamental sameness is embedded in the fact that they are all members of one species. But the bonds holding together the larger community of animals are based on something else: an acceptance of similarity over sameness and likeness over distinctness that allows them to find a means of navigation between the poles of identity and difference. Mr. Fox is the one to best articulate this paradigm of community formation, observing at one of the film's climactic moments that he sees before him a room full of "wild animals each with his own strengths and weaknesses due to his or her species. . . . I think it may very well be all the beautiful *differences* among us that just might give us the tiniest glimmer of a chance." It is an acceptance of being different *together* that gives the created community strength, a concept Mrs. Fox reiterates for Ash when he complains of feeling different from the other animals. "We *all* are . . . but there's something kind of fantastic about that, isn't there?" she explains, offering a flawless encapsulation of the idiosyncratic ideology of likeness that Flatley means to capture in the term "we-centricity."

To be sure, this bond of we-centricity does not allow the animals to miraculously rise above overwhelming circumstance and beat back the farmers and their machines, nor even to return in any way to the above-ground life they knew before. But it enables enough: It enables them to survive and endure in the face of enormous outside pressures. Together with Ash and Kylie, Mr. Fox manages to rescue Kristofferson, relying equally on the assorted strengths and wits of all involved. And by tunneling together and coordinating resources, the animals are able to create a new world deep underground where the farmers cannot get to them. It is impossible to tell whether the celebratory solution to the problem of survival that the film puts forward in its final frames is ultimately sustainable, with the animals finding a secret way into the Boggis, Bunce, and Bean supermarket and dancing for joy in the aisles. One imagines that their break-ins at the supermarket will ultimately be noticed and stopped in the same way that the break-ins at the farmhouses were. But regardless of the individual nature of the solution that is reached, the animal community has shown itself willing and able to work together across differences, finding its strength in discovered points of similarity rather than enforced notions of identity. The same is ultimately true of Mr. Fox's own family, which holds together in the face of great obstacles by coming to terms with difference and emphasizing likeness—accepting Felicity's powerful paradox of sameness in difference, celebrating the ways in which "we *all* are" different. Mr. Fox must of necessity no longer regard himself as quite so fantastic or exceptional, though in a truer sense than Royal could ever lay claim to he has every right to share his name with those around him, to consider each of his family members to be, in their own way, fantastic.

Shelf 2: Anderson's Faux Families

Rushmore (1998)   Anderson's triptych of family films, *Tenenbaums*, *Darjeeling*, and *Fox*, engage in an exploration of the ways in which families can either come together or break apart in the face of inside and outside pressures and traumas, meditating on the emotional afterlives of such cleavages. But interspersed chronologically with these pictures is another group of films that considers the fate of characters left outside any functional family structures, isolated individuals attempting to charm or cheat their way back into something that resembles a working kinship unit. Rather than exploring the difficulty of finding one's proper place within the given collection that is one's biological or adoptive family, these films follow characters who feel left outside the collected unit of the nuclear family and respond by trying to curate a constructed family unit of their own. Anderson's career begins with such a consideration, the three central friends of *Bottle Rocket* imperfectly forming what Orgeron calls an "ad-hoc familial community" (50). Yet it is arguably his second, *Rushmore*, that offers Anderson's paradigmatic examination of these issues. It is important to note that *Rushmore*'s central hero, Max Fischer (Jason Schwartzman), is not without family of his own. Though his mother died when he was seven years old, his father remains loving, and the two share a modest but warmly appointed home. Yet Max, whether by actual intellectual inclination or just pseudo-intellectual affectation, feels an unbridgeable distance from his biological father, and much of the film's narrative involves his pursuit of an alternate family structure more in keeping with his aggrandized self-image. "My top schools where I want to apply to are Oxford and the Sorbonne. But my safety is Harvard," he proudly declares at one point in the film, whereas his father is a humble barber who seems perfectly content with his unambitious but stable existence.

For most of the film, Max unapologetically writes his actual father out of existence, concocting fanciful tales of a neurosurgeon dad who is always on call and refusing to introduce his father to anyone when he does show up at school functions. Max effectively imagines his way into a kind of semiorphan status and then sets about trying to rectify his own self-imposed sense of missing family.

This is in large part a response to the overwhelming trauma of his mother's death. Max treats his loss quite casually at times in the film, offhandedly explaining to the widow Rosemary Cross (Olivia Williams) that "She died when I was seven. . . . So we both have dead people in our families." But like the traumatic separation of the Tenenbaum parents, this is a wound that for Max has never healed but only become fossilized. Whether by choice or circumstance, Max and his father live directly next door to the cemetery where his mother is buried, and Max visits her gravesite regularly. He is even shown setting up his precious typewriter outside in the family yard, with the cemetery in full view just on the other side of his home's chain-link fence. That typewriter—inscribed with the message "Bravo, Max! Love, Mom"—was a gift from Max's mother, and to the extent that Max's cultural (and class) ambitions are not simply a product of his own creation, we can assume that they are a kind of inheritance from her. More important than the typewriter is Rushmore itself, which also was a gift given shortly before she died. Max recounts that he gained entry to the prestigious Rushmore Academy on scholarship after his mother sent the headmaster a play he had written in the second grade—"a little one-act about Watergate," as he recalls—which places his admission as occurring in the same year that she passed away. Presumably a woman of relatively humble means like her husband, Max's mother nevertheless bequeathed her son a world of great privilege and potentially unlimited opportunity.

The irony of that bequest is that for all of the community and tradition and special privilege that Rushmore offers, Max feels almost entirely alone there. Max has an absolutely fierce loyalty to the institution (he spends nearly the entire film in an embossed Rushmore blazer that no one else wears and that for all we know may be of his own original design), which quite obviously seems to be a transference of his attachment to his mother. But he does not seem to have any friends beyond his devoted lower-school mentee Dirk (Mason Gamble), his "chapel partner" who was long ago assigned to him in a kind of upper-school–lower-school mentorship program that only the two of them continue to take seriously. Max is frequently pictured alone or in stark separation from the others around him on the school grounds—providing the lone standing ovation in an auditorium full of students, set apart from his classmates in a ridiculous crossing-guard getup at dismissal time—clearly marking his sense of isolation in this supposedly tightly knit private community (fig. 17). Max's response to this isolation, like that of so many Anderson protagonists, is to collect. But Max's collector's impulse is of a particularly immaterial sort. Max has only a few prized possessions (his blazer, his typewriter), but he as an absolutely enormous portfolio of clubs to his name. From his position as the debate team captain to his station as the Rushmore Beekepers president, Max has spent his years at Rushmore amassing a dizzying array of eighteen extracurricular posts, each presented individually in the film in a series of meticulously arranged tableaux set to "Making Time" by The Creation in one of the most beloved and frequently referenced montages of Anderson's career.

Orgeron describes this montage of extracurricular images as a kind of displaced family album, "imaginary surrogates for the more traditional (and for Max, painfully incomplete) family portrait" (48). It cannot be ignored, though, that the bonds Max has formed with his fellow club members seem minimal to nonexistent. Aside from Dirk and the participants in the school plays Anderson depicts, we meet no members of any of these clubs nor does Max ever actually make any mention of his fellow participants. One wonders just how many of these extracurriculars

Figure 17. Max stands out at Rushmore

ever hold meetings that go beyond Dirk and Max. Most of the clubs seems to be collector's items only, activities designed not to be used but to be set carefully on the metaphorical shelf of Max's social life, token representations of all the ways in which he is supposedly talented and all the social networks of which he is supposedly a part. The only one of these activities in which Max seems at all invested are his plays, which are far closer to tableau pieces than to actual human dramas. With their plots borrowed or stolen from macho genre films (Rushmore Academy may be the only posh private school in history to have presented a stage adaptation of *Serpico*), the only real genius evidenced in Max's theatrical pastimes is scenographic. Densely packed with physical detail and marked by ingenious uses of forced perspective, Max's plays seem like elaborate life-sized versions of the kind of shoebox dioramas common to many childhoods. According to Benjamin, the child's impulse to perform and put on plays is close to the childhood impulse to collect, a means of controlling and revivifying our drab world along a controlling axis of similarity—these things are like each other, I am like this character. For the collector and the child alike, he writes, "his gift for seeing similarity is nothing but a rudiment of the once powerful compulsion to become similar and to behave mimetically" (720). For all their visual sophistication, Max's plays are as much evidence of a kind of stunted adolescence as is his obsessive collection of clubs. Max seems to honestly believe he can make something real just by making it seem real, which is always the thespian's conceit but is also one that Max problematically applies to everything from his constructed extracurricular social life to the very idea that a place as isolated and isolating for him as Rushmore Academy can ever feel like home just because he wears a blazer.

This interplay of collection and performance comes to a head in what is to be Max's greatest construction of the film, the alternate family he attempts to call into being through his relationships with Rosemary Cross and Herman Blume (Bill Murray). The initial impulse behind this effort is supposedly romantic. Max is teased by the other boys at school for his lack of sexual accomplishment and seems to take their empty adolescent taunts and boasts as the impetus for yet another mission, engaging in a bizarre and one-sided courtship with Rosemary, a teacher in Rushmore's lower school, by way of a series of grand misguided gestures, rescuing the school's Latin curriculum because of a collegiate interest in Latin American politics that she offhandedly recalls and attempting to commission the construction of a Rushmore aquarium because she has decorated her classroom with fish tanks. If Rosemary is supposed to be an actual romantic partner for Max in any way, she is a romantic partner of a particularly Oedipal sort. She neither is conventionally attractive in the way that might impress hormonal teenage boys nor shows any particularly amorous response to Max's advances besides a kind of incredulous curiosity at his audacity. What she is, is a figure affiliated with and approved by Max's beloved Rushmore, which serves as an institutional stand-in for his deceased mother, and a kind of motherlike figure in her own right yet without any children of her own. Rosemary teaches first grade, which would have been the last full year of Max's life that he spent with his mother before she died in his second-grade year. Indeed, when Max sees Rosemary for the very first time in the film, she is reading aloud to a group of children gathered at her feet, hardly the kind of activity that might excite the libido of most teenagers. Max's interest in sexuality is minimal at best—he is completely clueless about the advances of a fellow public schooler later in the film and only half-heartedly interested in reciprocating once her attraction dawns on him. But his interest in identifying a substitute mother figure is understandable and profound.

Paired to Rosemary in Max's imagined family unit is the steel tycoon and Rushmore benefactor Herman Blume, whose wealth and prestige offer to Max everything that his loving but unassuming father cannot. It also doesn't hurt that Herman is just about the only adult male figure in the film who does not find Max's pushiness and affectation totally exasperating. "He's a sharp little guy," Herman observes after meeting Max for the first time, to which the tormented school headmaster, the figure tasked with continually warning Max of his potential expulsion for poor grades on account of his extracurricular excesses, can only reply "He's one of the worst students we've got." Linked together by their shared interest in Max and his activities, Max's Rushmore-approved surrogate father and Rushmore-approved surrogate mother—representing a classically gendered separation of breadwinning and caretaking—visually function like a family unit through much of the film, as when the two of them sit together with Max's surrogate younger brother Dirk in the bleachers of a public school gymnasium and watch Max perform as a male cheerleader like proud (if somewhat bemused) parents. That Max essentially views his elected adults in this way is made most clear by the emotional temper-tantrum he throws when Rosemary invites a male friend from college along to an elegant dinner that is supposed to be only for Max and Rosemary and Herman after the premier of one of his school plays. Rosemary's friend John (Luke Wilson) is ostensibly a romantic threat to Max, though there is no real indication here or elsewhere in the film that the two old college friends have any actual romantic involvement. And if this were actually supposed to be a kind of date with Rosemary, one wonders what Herman was ever doing there. Rather, Max's evening out was supposed to be a celebratory dinner with his surrogate parents—one to which his actual father was pointedly not invited—and John's presence destroys the conceit. Hitting John with a spoon and pushing dinnerware at him, Max begins acting like a child, which in some ways was always exactly the point.

Bad behavior aside, most adults would hardly tolerate the kind of extrafamilial attachment that Max carefully orchestrates throughout the film, and the degree to which Herman and Rosemary consent to Max's filial advances is a measure of their reciprocal isolation and desperation within failed family units of their own. *Rushmore* in fact opens with a disturbing oil portrait of the Blume family, Herman set deliberately to the side smoking a cigarette with his melancholic wife and two angry adolescent boys featured behind him. Early in the film we are given indications of his wife's rather obvious extramarital flirtations and possible affairs when she and another man flagrantly feed each other fruit in full view of Herman during his twin sons' birthday party, a fact that seems to bother Herman not nearly as much as does the sheer brutishness of the children whose birthday he is supposed to be celebrating. "Never in my wildest imagination did I ever dream I would have sons like these," he confesses to Max. A self-made millionaire, Herman somewhat gallingly uses his Rushmore chapel speech near the opening of the film to urge the scholarship students in the school to "take dead aim on the rich boys. Get them in the crosshairs. And take them down," essentially pitting students like Max against Blume's own overly privileged offspring. Herman's isolation and existential anguish are cemented in an early visual allusion to *The Graduate* that inverts the generational gap of that film—alone and curled into a fetal position underneath the water of his backyard pool during his sons' celebration, it is now the aging and ostensibly successful baby boomer who feels alienated from the very world and the very family he has made for himself. With this as his troubled home life, Herman gladly accepts the alternate family structure that Max has created for him.

Rosemary's relationship to Max's advances is more complicated, in that her familial isolation stems, like Max's own, from an unresolved emotional trauma more than it is a product of alienation or ennui. Rosemary came to teach at Rushmore after the premature death of her husband Edward Appleby, who had once been a student there. Like Max, her attachment to the institution is born of displacement, the Rushmore community offering a form of connection to a loved one who has passed away. Though Rosemary's connection to Rushmore is far more tenuous than Max's fanatical devotion and she in fact resigns her position as a way of escaping Max's continued advances, her frozen-in-amber relationship to the trauma of her husband's death is arguably every bit as potent as Max's maternal heartache. "She's in love with a dead guy," Herman dismissively says when he learns of Rosemary's past, though his flip diagnosis does not even begin to scratch the surface of her ongoing relationship with Edward. Claiming to be "just kind of housesitting," Rosemary is in fact living in her dead husband's childhood home while teaching at the school that he once attended. We eventually learn that she has even moved into his childhood room and sleeps in his childhood twin bed, having left the room exactly as it was during Edward's boyhood, model airplane collection and all. "You live in his room, with all his stuff," Max points out to her incredulously in one of their confrontations. For her, Max must appear as some kind of apparition of a past that she never directly knew but wants to somehow connect to. "You remind me of him, you know," she says. She seems to have come to Edward's home town looking for such ghosts.

Max's constructed family manages to function as such only briefly— that short scene in the high school gymnasium is just about the only time one of their gatherings does not descend into emotional disaster—and only insofar as it remains chaste, which is the childhood understanding of family life. Herman's halting courtship of Rosemary, which in effect Max set in motion by pairing them as his surrogate parents, is taken by Max as a kind of grand betrayal of his designs, a moment when the diorama has become too lifelike. The discovery of Herman and Rosemary's relationship exposes the conceit to which Max was still clutching that his interest in Rosemary was more sweetly romantic than cloyingly filial, with Herman merely present to all their encounters and dates as some kind of neutral third-party witness. Having set in place a surrogate family like so many characters in one of his curio-cabinet theater pieces, Max discovers to his own horror that he has also set in motion a kind of surrogate Oedipal drama. Hence the long portion of the film given over to Max and Herman's *Looney Tunes*–like tit-for-tat, wherein the violent stakes grow ever higher but the actual consequences remain negligible: Max releases a swarm of bees into the hotel room Herman has moved into upon finally separating from his wife; Herman runs over Max's bicycle multiple times with his car; Max cuts Herman's brakes, though the resulting crash is mostly harmless. As a culmination, Max even tries to finagle a cartoonlike tripwire that would cause a tree to fall on Herman and, in the millionaire's own words, "would have flattened me like a pancake." But instead they declare a truce, agreed to on the site of Max's mother's grave—the origin point back to which all of Max's antics can be traced. Max and Herman finally realize that their conflict has become pointless, as Rosemary has simply used it as an opportunity to resign her part as substitute wife-mother-object of desire, quietly deaccessioning herself from Max's collection of family members and disappearing.

She does not appear again until the very end of the film, when the promise of a new Max Fischer Production manages to coax her into attendance—a feat not even Max and Herman's renewed attempt to build her an aquarium was able to do, though Herman claims to have spent eight million dollars on the quixotic venture. Max attempts to use his latest play as a means of setting back in place all the pieces of his life he had tried to rearrange in the months before. He dedicates the performance "to the memory of my mother, Eloise Fischer," acknowledging her by name for the first time in the film and through that acknowledgment releasing Rosemary from the surrogate role into which she had been cast, and adds a second dedication, "To Edward Appleby. A friend of a friend," recognizing publicly Rosemary's own trauma and relinquishing the tacit claim he held on taking over the position of her own figure of loss—whether as her lover, in Edward's adult manifestation, or as the child for whom she has clearly gone seeking in coming to Edward's childhood home. The ending tableau of the film, set at a dance following the play, carefully arranges the main characters in the way that Max might most like to display them were they his collectibles—at the center, he is dancing with Rosemary, but the arrangement at least acknowledges the transpositions taking place: to the right Herman is dancing with Max's new girlfriend, to the left Max's actual father dances with Max's public-school mathematics teacher. The pairings are only temporary and can be changed. Most important, everyone has a place.

The Life Aquatic with Steve Zissou (2004)   There are perhaps no two films in the Anderson canon that seem more unlike one another than *Rushmore* and *The Life Aquatic*, the former a relatively intimate examination of life at a sequestered private academy that is among the director's more visually understated films, and the other an epic high-seas adventure involving pirates, gun battles, and an elusive giant beast called the jaguar shark that is among Anderson's most spectacularly fantastical works. There is a kind of joking connection between the two in the copy of *Diving for Sunken Treasure* by Jacques Cousteau that Max discovers in the Rushmore library and that eventually leads him to Rosemary, but mostly *The Life Aquatic* seems like a Max Fischer Production come vividly to life, visually dense and emotionally immature. Of course, Max would have set his version of the story in the heyday of Captain Steve Zissou's (Bill Murray) career, when funding for his deep-sea adventure documentaries came easily and his films were all hits. Anderson is interested in the twilight of this niche celebrity life and the ways in which the exigencies of time and trauma take their toll on those who are only used to success. Zissou is in possession of the kind of constructed family unit about which Max could only dream: a close-knit team of deep-water adventurers who have long lived life as a collective unit, a group of unrelated adults who earnestly speak of themselves as being brothers and sisters, parents and children to one another. The challenge Team Zissou must face is in many ways the opposite of that which Max poses to Herman and Rosemary. Presenting himself with some degree of possible legitimacy as Zissou's long-lost son, Ned Plimpton (Owen Wilson) disrupts Zissou's assembled family with his claim of actual kinship and his entreaty that Zissou take on the actual role of father after a lifetime of serving only as a kind of surrogate father-figure, both to his team and to his fans. The confusing clash of kinship and collectivity that marked the central relationships in *Rushmore* here appears again with the emphasis only slightly shifted: The question is not whether an alternate family structure can be built at all but whether such alternate-family collectives once achieved can sustain themselves in the face of external pressures and internal disruptions—and at what costs. "I hate fathers and I never wanted to be one," Zissou insists, and only slowly over the course of the film does he come to realize that one is not always given a choice.

Of course, for a figure who supposedly hates fathers as much as Zissou, he certainly has no trouble playing one in the movies. The world-wide Zissou phenomenon that Anderson asks us to accept as a basic premise of the film—a kind of fanciful imagination of a world in which a Cousteau-like figure could today equally command the affection of a global children's fan club and the esteem of European film festivals—seems to be based largely on the appeal of the constructed family unit of Team Zissou, with Zissou himself as its benevolent captain and *pater familias*. The old Zissou films that we are able to glimpse briefly during Anderson's movie actually look quite dull and poorly executed as cinematic objects, but they also look like they were a great deal of fun to make. Splashing playfully in icy pools of arctic water together, rescuing adorable marine mammals as a team: The real appeal of these films seems to lie in the simple thrills they depicted and the vicarious camaraderie they offered—camaraderie that was directly extended to the fans by way of the Zissou Society and by Zissou's commitment to answering letters personally from as many of his young admirers as he could. More than entertainment, the Zissou enterprise seemed to offer a window into a certain kind of group experience. It certainly didn't offer much in the way of education, despite its quasi-scientific pretenses. One of the running gags of Anderson's film is Zissou's notably poor command of scientific facts. He knows a few pieces of information about each creature that he and his team encounter, but scratch below his prepared statements, as Ned innocently starts to do when he joins the team, and you very quickly reach the outer limits of Zissou's actual scientific knowledge. Fundamentally, Zissou is a collector: an appreciator of the natural world perpetually delighted by the discovery and filmic acquisition of new items but a figure of very limited practical knowledge. By his own admission, he doesn't actually "have the background" for the job. "No one here does," he says. But that lack of knowledge seems to be a large part of his allure. For Stewart, the true collector is always limited in his or her real understanding of the objects being collected—their appeal must lie in the magic that they add to the collection as a whole rather than the specifics of their existence outside that collection. As she writes, "a 'formal' interest always replaces a 'real' interest in collected objects" (154), such that the collector "ignores properties of native history and topography" (153). The power of the collector is in the order that he or she bestows on things, not the knowledge of them that he or she imparts. Hence the appeal that Zissou seems to hold as a childhood celebrity figure in particular. To children and to the childlike, Zissou brings order to the world around them without any sacrifice of wonder: with each animal that he encounters he offers a name and a little information, but mostly he just marvels at its beauty. In contrast to the collections of the traumatized figures that mark so many of Anderson's films, this is the collection of the happy child who innocently uses the imposition of order and arrangement as a chance to refresh the world and to make it his or her own. The magic of the Zissou phenomenon is that he is both father and child at once, both a figure of authority to his comrades and his club members and a fellow kid crawling around the backyard along with them.

Or at least that was Zissou in his heyday. As the reporter Jane Winslett-Richardson (Cate Blanchett) says reflecting back on her youthful love of all things Zissou, "The Zissou of my childhood represents all the dreams I've come to regret." The whole world seems to have moved beyond the insistent and arguably self-indulgent innocence of Zissou's floating society, with Zissou's producer complaining that "we haven't made a hit documentary in nine years" and all his sources of funding now drying up. All the grant money, Zissou claims, now goes to his competitor Alistair Hennessey (Jeff Goldblum), who might be tying up all the funding dollars but certainly hasn't encroached on Zissou's brand space: slick and highly polished, he seems like an affluent yachtsman to Zissou's affable tugboat captain. Zissou has no ready answer to Jane's pointed question of "What happened?" though he cannot disagree with her assessment that "the public perception of your work has altered in the last five years." The world seemed to grow up around him, while he and his crew remained stuck in the stunted adolescence in which so many Anderson characters linger. Their more recent films certainly seem no better or worse than those for which they were once world-famous. Watching old episodes of Team Zissou's adventures, Zissou's compatriot Klaus (Willem Dafoe) doesn't lament the quality of the films they once were able to make but the quality of who they themselves used to be. "That's what it used to be like," he says sadly as a younger version of himself gallivants around the screen in a mohawk.

This general loss of innocence is crystallized for Zissou in the tragic death of his longtime exploring partner Esteban du Plantier (Seymour Cassel), killed in the middle of a shoot by a quasi-mythical creature for which Zissou invents the name jaguar shark; the footage from the fatal expedition, screened at a film festival in the fictional Italian city of Loquasto, opens Anderson's picture. To lose one's best friend during a tragic documentary shoot and then to have that same documentary poorly received upon its release is perhaps some special version of the documentarian's worst nightmare, a situation that is made even worse for Zissou by the fact that many in the audience seem to doubt whether the elusive jaguar shark is even real. One cannot really blame these doubters, and although Anderson actually shows us the jaguar shark at the end of the film, he still does not entirely answer the question. Like the giant bulldozers in *Fantastic Mr. Fox* or the man-eating tiger in *The Darjeeling Limited*, the film's fantastical shark seems less like a real, live beast than a physical manifestation of the emotional desolation that experience inevitably brings to Anderson's slow-to-mature characters or a consolidation of the abstract forces of dispersion with which so many Anderson figures struggle. All the fantastical creatures that Zissou discovers in the film, from the candy-cane-colored sugar crabs to the Crayola-bright crayon ponyfish, seem like figments of a child's imagination, the giant luminescent jaguar shark being only their darker, more nightmarish cousin. Zissou's enterprise was in decline long before the trauma of Esteban's death, and it is unclear whether this event alone is what brought childhood's end. What is certain is that the Zissou who sets out from Loquasto to make his final film is different, angrier, and less benevolent than the figure that we glimpse in those earlier movies or in the refracted image projected back by his adoring child fans. Zissou, that great filmic collector of the natural world who once cradled baby mongoose pups in the palms of his hands to the delight of children everywhere, now has taken as his last mission the destruction of the rare sea creature that killed his friend. "Now I'm going to hunt down that shark or whatever it is, and, hopefully, kill it. I don't know how yet, maybe dynamite," he tells the assembled glitterati at the film gala. It is a mission about as sensible as Ahab's.

But it is not the hardest mission that Zissou will face in the film. That distinction belongs to the request that an unassuming airline pilot from Kentucky makes of the great explorer during an on-board party after the screening. "You're supposed to be my son, right?" Zissou asks after learning who Ned's mother was. "I don't know," Ned replies. "But I did want to meet you, just in case." For a long-lost son who has undertaken a journey across an ocean in order to meet a father he has never known, Ned is remarkably understated and unassuming in his interactions, even after Zissou essentially backs up the likely legitimacy of his claims. "I don't want to take up any more of your time," he says after only a brief conversation. "Thank you very much for talking to me." Ned's journey is not unlike that of the Whitman brothers in *The Darjeeling Limited*: His mother has just recently committed suicide after a long battle with cancer, and it is only in the wake of that death that he has thought to seek out the man who may be his only remaining relative. But unlike Francis and Jack and Peter, Ned makes no demands of spiritual awakening or special acceptance from his one living parent, instead asking only for some token recognition. He doesn't even want to stay in Italy that long, explaining "I have to be back in Kentucky on Thursday" when Zissou makes the grand gesture of inviting Ned to his private island.

So it is perhaps all the more surprising the depths to which Ned's appearance shakes the once unflappable adventurer. Zissou and Ned have met at a point equidistant from their respective recent tragedies, the deaths of Esteban and Ned's mother both set in the very recent past, but their reactions to their joint encounter could not be more different. Ned, who is now effectively familyless, asks for nothing but acknowledgment; he has his job and his life back home—indeed, he arrives on Zissou's boat in his pilot's uniform, a beacon of his collective professional identity—and is willing to accept them as sufficient. Zissou possesses a surrogate family as close as any in Anderson's body of films:

a team of seven co-adventurers who seem to live with him year-round and who have no identifiable attachments outside their life with Team Zissou. Yet it is a family facing a possibly immanent disarray. Zissou's wife Eleanor is clearly disaffected by her husband's professional decline, and Zissou worries that she may leave him. The difficulty of securing funding threatens to rob Zissou's team of the missions that give their life together purpose. And the death of Esteban has left the very structure of Team Zissou open to a kind of renegotiation the explorer has never faced before. Viewed in this context, Zissou's fateful and somewhat impulsive decision to invite Ned to join his exploring team is as much a bid to save Team Zissou itself as it is to reconnect with a long-lost son, an attempt to inject new life into the failing operation and at the same time cement Zissou's place as surrogate father to the other team members by literalizing that position via Ned. "It's the Steve Zissou show, not the Ned show. You hear me?" Klaus says in a highly emotional moment of confrontation with the surprise new member of the ensemble. It seems on the surface like a comically drastic overreaction, but Klaus is not wrong to suspect the new orientation of the group. Zissou's paradoxical adoption of his biological son into his constructed family unit is not an entirely benign event, and Ned is not necessarily on a level with the other members of the team—if not by virtue of his kinship ties then certainly by virtue of the fact that he volunteers his inheritance to help fund Zissou's last film, the personal and the financial always being for Zissou almost impossible to untwine. "This one was my son. Also our equity partner," Zissou says by way of introducing Ned to his viewership after his tragic death later in the film, unable or unwilling to separate or hierarchize the various aspects of their relationship.

With Ned now added to the team, the question then becomes what exactly that team will be. Zissou's impulse is to strip Ned of his preexisting identity and insert him as seamlessly as possible into the Team Zissou collective. By way of accepting Ned into his seagoing family, Zissou says simply "I'll order you a red cap and a Speedo," and Ned is quickly outfitted in the requisite light blue suit. When Ned balks at the idea that he is supposed to wear a handgun strapped ostentatiously to his thigh at all times, Zissou insists that the newcomer adhere to the team's fashion and weaponry codes. "No exceptions," he says. What Zissou is essentially trying to enforce, somewhat paradoxically considering his status as a professional collector of wondrous creatures, is an ideology of sameness, the individual identities of the Team Zissou members all subsumed under the greater identity of the Zissou brand. Zissou himself has long made his living and his name by showing his fans the wonders of similarity and likeness, gaping at the beauties of the creatures he discovers while imbuing them with the mark of similarity that comes from being part of his collected world. Through their differences, they are all in some way alike. Yet Zissou clearly does not extend this more open view of connectivity to the professional family he has gathered around him, whom he dresses identically to himself and to whom he relates largely interchangeably. Zissou's team is notably diverse in its ethnic, racial, and national makeup as befits a global enterprise, counting among its members a German engineer, an Afro-Brazilian safety expert, an Indian cameraman, a Japanese diver, an Italian film editor, a Russian-Jewish score composer, and an American script supervisor. Yet there is an almost disconcerting flatness and fungibility to the team members, as a number of commentators have observed. The members of Team Zissou, Dean-Ruzicka writes, "are used to populate the landscape rather than participate in the actual story itself in any meaningful way" (35). Some critics have taken this aspect of the film as evidence of Anderson's problematic relationship with race as a filmmaker, what Weiner calls "the clumsy, discomfiting way he stages interactions between white protagonists . . . and nonwhite foils." But this flattening of the Team Zissou members also is arguably an important diegetic feature of the film, a measure of the degree to which Zissou has somewhat disturbingly stripped his teammates of their individual preexisting identities as a condition of entry into his collective in the same way that he attempts to strip Ned of his.

The difference is that Ned—whether through the assumed privilege of his kinship tie to Zissou or the hasty and improvisational nature of his addition to the team or just simple ignorance—does not understand Zissou's demands for sameness or the hierarchical assumptions that they reveal underneath the supposed egalitarianism of those corny matching jumpsuits. In ways both large and small, Ned begins to subtly but surely undercut the long-established working methods of the team and the demands of conformity that they enforce. Ad-libbing lines during takes and asking simple questions of Zissou on camera that the great oceanographer cannot answer, Ned essentially makes a general nuisance of himself within the highly codified world into which he has stumbled. "Steve, what produces this effect of illumination? Is there a chemical inside the organism?" he asks impromptu during one filming, forcing Steve to rummage through his limited scientific knowledge on the spot. But there is no greater expression of his assumed privilege within the group and obliviousness to the conformism of the clan he has joined than his sudden request "for me to address you as Dad in this scene," a question posed after Zissou has already ordered the cameras to start rolling. Zissou is aghast and quickly replies "No," reluctantly adding "It's not a bad impulse, though. Some kind of nickname. Not that one. It's too specific, but try to think of something else." He himself suggests "Stevesy" as a possible alternative nickname, knowing full well that it is a ridiculous substitution; he later changes it to the slightly less unintimate but infinitely more ridiculous "Papa Steve." Zissou clearly has trouble with the vocabulary of fatherhood, not just with Ned but with all his team members. Trying to reassure Klaus about the special position he still holds in the team after Ned's entry, Zissou tells him that "me and Esteban always thought of you as our baby brother." Klaus responds with a more intimate assessment of the relationship (and one that acknowledges the obvious homoerotic aspects of Team Zissou's former dual-parental manifestation), claiming "I've always thought of you two as my dads," but Zissou has nothing to say in answer to this suggestion of faux paternity.

It would be one thing if Zissou's father aversion were based on an honestly felt and truly radical egalitarianism—if he actually meant that he saw the members of Team Zissou as being all brothers and sisters with no degrees of hierarchy to divide them. But Zissou clearly does not mean anything of the sort. He merely means to obfuscate the entirely one-sided power dynamics of the Zissou clan. Like Royal before him and Mr. Fox after him, Zissou claims the privileges of the father position without acknowledging any of its reciprocal responsibilities. He decides unilaterally who will be adopted into the surrogate family, and he even exercises the privilege of renaming them, drawing up stationary for Ned that reads "Kingsley (Ned) Zissou," Kingsley being the name Zissou thinks he would have given to his son had he known he had one. Perhaps most egregiously, Zissou exercises the parental monopoly on sexuality within the family and "claims" Jane as his potential conquest when she joins Team Zissou on their ship, specifically instructing Klaus to stay away from her and wantonly ignoring the not insignificant fact that he himself is already married. Jane, of course, has no particular care for Zissou's expressions of sexual property and no more interest in working through any residual Elektral issues with this surrogate father figure than Rosemary had of working through Max's Oedipal impulses in *Rushmore*. Single and five months pregnant by a married man, Jane is by her own description somewhat urgently in need of an actual father figure for her unborn son, and she sees Ned as a plausible candidate. Like some generationally inverted version of Max Fischer, Zissou chooses to see this perfectly legitimate and actually age-appropriate relationship as a major betrayal of his created family along the lines of how Max saw the courtship of Herman and Rosemary. Yet neither Jane nor Ned is able to parse Zissou's objections or understand why exactly he thinks he has standing to raise them, Jane having never consented to join the Zissou family and Ned still understanding only imperfectly how that family is supposed to work. Jane insists, quite reasonably, that it's "none of your business" how she conducts her romantic life, and Ned protests on a technicality and points out "You said, 'Not this one, Klaus,'" not understanding Zissou's prerogative to enforce a general sexual prohibition.

For Zissou, this perceived betrayal between father and son is enough to end their just-started relationship and tear the new version of Team Zissou apart. "Don't you dare put on that uniform," he tells Ned after discovering him with Jane. Ironically enough, Ned's actions do precipitate the dissolution of the team in the most literal of ways: skipping out on his responsibility to man the watch so that he can sleep with Jane in her cabin, Ned fails to notice that the *Belafonte* is about to be boarded by pirates. The pirate attack is one of the stranger moments in Anderson's filmmaking, not just because the level of verisimilitude depicted in the early stages of the hijacking has no parallel in his films but also because that verisimilitude so quickly vanishes. Working his way loose from the ropes that are binding him, Zissou effectively scares the heavily armed pirates away mostly by yelling at them. Firing his handgun wildly around the deck and haranguing the intruders in something like the manner of mad King Lear screaming at the storm, Zissou somehow inveighs these evil spirits to leave. The moment is not so much fantastical as dreamlike, the pirates representing not an actual maritime threat so much as a manifestation of the forces of disruption that Zissou has long feared would beset his carefully preserved floating world and that Ned somehow unleashed upon the Zissou family unit by challenging the parental prerogative and sexual privilege of its father figure. Team Zissou will never be the same after the attack, for although the pirates appeared suddenly in a cloud of haze and disappeared just as suddenly in a barrage of screaming, the damage that they wrought was very real: a kidnapped film financier, a badly bloodied intern, and a terribly traumatized crew for whom the handguns on their thighs were mostly supposed to be for decoration. Three members of Zissou's crew plus all but one of his interns quit after the attack, bringing Zissou's worst fears to pass about the destruction of the family he has tried so hard to build—and to control—for so long. He assumes that his seafaring and filmmaking days are no more, which is a reasonable assumption because he has now officially run out of money.

What changes Zissou's mind is a telephone call—a brief message from the bond company employee who was kidnapped by the pirates trying to provide clues to his location. It is in one sense a classic hero opportunity, a chance for Zissou to set out on a bold and clear mission and to win back some degree of paternal bona fides by way of martial prowess, reasserting his authority both to himself and to his crew. But there is actually a less self-serving element in Zissou's change of heart as well, a shift within him that is more epistemic than emotional. "I've never seen a bond company stooge stick his neck out like that," he declares after the insurance man takes Ned's place as the pirate's hostage. Zissou sees something new in the character he has always simply called the "bond company stooge," something that makes him begin to rethink his attachment to the category of sameness on which he has premised the construction of Team Zissou. Zissou always assumed there was a kernel of identity that bound together the select individuals he allowed into his family of seafarers. "We're a pack of strays," he says proudly at one point, a group of lonesome outsiders brought together by a quality that Esteban in one old episode calls simply "Zissou." And if there was ever a character lacking in that effervescent quality, Zissou believed it to be the short, rotund, balding, and generally nebbishy "bond company stooge" that his financial backers forced him to bring along on his journey for insurance reasons. Nevertheless, that supposed stooge, though physically and dispositionally far from the elect Olympians of Team Zissou, has proved himself to have more pluck and resourcefulness than many of Zissou's own chosen compatriots. Not that Zissou would ever think to offer him a red cap and a Speedo, but neither would he need to. In the wake of his cherished family's breakup and near-demise, Zissou has come to recognize in the people around him the same wondrous value of similarity and likeness he has always seen in the natural world that he studies. The bond company representative may not be in the same species or the same genus as Klaus or Vikram, but there is something remarkable about him nonetheless: certainly enough to include him in the same family.

The version of Team Zissou that emerges in the aftermath of the remaining crew's rescue of the bond man—perhaps the most hapless commando operation of all time—is a different animal, so to speak, from the conformist entity over which Zissou had previously presided. Here at last is something closer to the inclusive and beneficent group that Zissou's open and wondrous attitude toward the natural world would seem to suggest, a group brought together by a logic of similarity rather than sameness, by an ethos of we-centricity. Here at last the bond company rep has been welcomed into the fold; Zissou's wife Eleanor, who bankrolled and brainstormed the rescue operation after previously flirting with leaving the group for good, has rejoined; Zissou's producer is there, as is the man who has been hogging all the grant money, Alistair Hennessey, rescued unexpectedly along with the bond company representative from the kidnapping pirates. When Ned redesigns the Team Zissou flag in the wake of the group's new formation, he does so in a way that reflects the newfound ethos of actual collectivity, replacing the triple Z of the old insignia and its enforced iteration of the central Zissou identity with a patchwork design that includes iconographic references to multiple team members, Klaus and Esteban included, as well as a "circle [that] represents friendship."

The dark irony of this wholesale renovation of Team Zissou's collective identity is that in the end it can do nothing to stave off trauma and pain. The world is still the world, and experience is inevitable; innocence cannot last forever. No sooner does Ned make a gift of the reformulated flag to his new teammates than he and Zissou take off on a helicopter flight in search of the jaguar shark that results in Ned's sudden death when the unmaintained chopper blades give out. Now one single semi-mythical beast has been the cause, directly or indirectly, of the deaths of the two men closest to Zissou, his husband-brother Esteban and his partner-son Ned, lending credence to the idea that the shark is not so much a rare marine creature as a deep-sea embodiment of death itself, a force against which no family can protect itself. But whereas the family he has built and now allowed to blossom all around him cannot save Zissou, it can salve him. Diving deep into the ocean in the *Belafonte's* submersible just days after Ned's death, a shell-shocked Zissou and the ragtag crew he has left finally encounter the jaguar shark face to face again. Zissou no longer wants to kill the beast, asking only "I wonder if he remembers me." Like Ned when he first came to meet his likely father, Zissou now wants only to be recognized. In a dreamlike moment that follows, one by one the members of the new and newly expanded Team Zissou family lay their hands on Zissou until they are all touching him together. Zissou reaches out to touch Jane's pregnant belly and Jane, apropos of nothing, remarks that "in twelve years he'll be eleven and a half." "That was my favorite age," Zissou says. The world can still be full of wonder at age eleven and a half and full of warmth and safety too if one is lucky enough to have a loving family. Zissou has managed at last to find both.

Bottle Rocket (1996)   Though it has arguably taken him the better part of his adult life to fully achieve, the constructed family that Zissou builds in *The Life Aquatic* and that supports him as he confronts the specter of mortality that appears before him in the deep is perhaps the most successful example of a constructed familial collective in Anderson's body of films. But the desire to build such a unit in the face of a profound breakdown of the biological family runs all the way back to the director's very first film. Before Zissou set off to sea with his ragtag band of loyal sailor-kin and before Max Fischer tried to cobble a steel magnate and a first-grade teacher into an alternate parental pair, the three lead characters of *Bottle Rocket* attempted to build a kind of forced brotherhood in the gaping absence of any actual family ties. These thematic similarities notwithstanding, *Bottle Rocket* has always made an odd fit with Anderson's other works: It is the least invested in what would become his trademark visual style and the most connected to certain cinematic trends prevalent in mid-1990s independent cinema that would ultimately have little place in Anderson's other works—stories of hip gangsterism in the vein of Quentin Tarantino's *Reservoir Dogs* or picaresque tales of juvenile and young adult high jinks in the manner of Kevin Smith's *Clerks* and *Mallrats*. It also is, not incidentally, the film over which Anderson had the least amount of direct creative control, with Columbia Pictures executives demanding test screenings and rewrites throughout postproduction. As producer James L. Brooks lamented around that time, "This personal, spirited, original piece of work was walking exactly the same market testing plank as big Hollywood genre pics" (x). It also is the film that enabled all the others, winning just enough critical acclaim for Anderson to allow him to find studio support for a new film he and Owen Wilson were working on called *Rushmore*.

In fact, the whole story of Anderson's creative journey in making *Bottle Rocket* is so fantastical that it almost seems like something out of one of his later films—a fantasy of automatic success and acclaim along the lines of Max's geometry-classroom dream sequence in *Rushmore* or the tales of the young Tenenbaums' instantaneous professional triumphs at the start of that film. Anderson and fellow classmate Owen Wilson began writing the script for *Bottle Rocket* while they were still undergraduates at the University of Texas at Austin and then put together enough money to make a thirteen-minute short-form version of the film while living together in Dallas after graduation. With no formal film training to speak of (Anderson was a philosophy major, Wilson studied English), the two saw their first cinematic effort accepted at Sundance and quickly started fielding telephone calls from Hollywood producers, including industry icon James L. Brooks. Only a few years out of college, the pair found themselves with a deal from Columbia to turn *Bottle Rocket* into a feature-length film. From there their fortunes sank somewhat, though only briefly. The feature-length version of the picture was rejected by every major film festival in which they tried to enter it, and many critics responded to the oddball heist movie with pure puzzlement. Critic David Hinckley in the *New York Daily News*, for instance, predicted that the film would hold little appeal for anyone besides its quirky creators, writing "*Bottle Rocket* was conceived as a low-budget family affair . . . and outside a few cult-intensive pockets of fandom, that's where it's likely to end up." But some important critical voices saw something worthwhile in the film, spearheaded in particular by *Los Angeles Times* critic Kenneth Turan, who called it "a confident, eccentric debut . . . [that] feels particularly refreshing because it never compromises on its delicate deadpan sensibility." In Brooks's estimation, "The Turan review . . . without exaggeration saved Wes and Owen's lives" (xii). In retrospect, aspects of this initial enthusiasm can seem a little misguided. Martin Scorsese, for instance, declared Anderson to be "the next Martin Scorsese," a claim which would later come to border on the surreal in light of the reputation Anderson developed as a kind of modern troubadour of twee. Yet there were still important elements of the later Anderson in that early effort, which the director himself refuses to separate from his other works. "I always have the same approach," he says when asked to define what makes his early film different (qtd. in Seitz 58). Scorsese may actually not have been too far off the mark in identifying some kernel of connection between his brutal visions of street life and Anderson's careful confections, even if the idea of a direct inheritance significantly overstates the case. "Wes Anderson . . . has a very special kind of talent: He knows how to convey the simple joys and interactions between people so well and with such richness," he explained, with no small amount of insight into how the director might later develop.

Arguably, the heart of this connection between the Anderson of *Bottle Rocket* and the Anderson of *Rushmore* and afterward lies in the director's native and largely unchanging interest in examining the dynamics of the disrupted family and the attempts of his characters to either formulate a fix or fashion a replacement. Or, as Mr. Henry (James Caan) puts it in *Bottle Rocket* when describing the predicament of Dignan (Owen Wilson), the boyish lost soul at the film's center, "Here he is, he thought he had a team. Turns out to be a man alone. That's tough now. Real tough." Many critical responses to *Bottle Rocket* have emphasized the film's interest in the corrosive effects of wealth and privilege, taking the disaffectedness of its upper-class suburbanite characters as central to understanding the hazily defined motivating force behind their ill-advised and poorly executed small-time crime spree—the first of many Anderson films, in one account, that "have concentrated on a group of insecure goofballs from wealthy backgrounds" ("How Did All That Movie Talent Crash.") There is certainly no shortage of privileged torpor in the film. Bob Mapplethorpe (Robert Musgrave), with no job and no need for one, lives in a perpetual state of moneyed languor, dividing his time between doing nothing in his parents' richly appointed home and doing nothing at the family country club. For Anthony (Luke Wilson), the apparent unavailability of meaningful activity in his life just about drives him crazy—or at least spurs him to voluntarily admit himself into a posh sanitarium. "One morning over at Elizabeth's beach house, she asked me if I'd rather go water-skiing or lay-out," he says, explaining his decision to resign from his own affluent lifestyle. "I realized that not only did I not want to answer that question, but I never wanted to answer another water sports question or see any of these people again for the rest of my life." Lurking behind these rather trite rich-kid complaints and their second-order Lloyd Dobler opt-outism is another factor that is arguably of far greater emotional weight within the film: the conspicuous absence of parents and the overall lack of any identifiable family structures.

Of course, Anderson's twenty-something protagonists are old enough to be living on their own and making their way in the world independent of immediate familial presence or support—as Anderson and Wilson themselves were doing at the time, holed up in Dallas and working on their film project. But none of Anderson's characters have made that departure. Rather, they are all still living in the town where they grew up, shuffling between the homes and businesses they have always known. And although their shared milieu remains unchanged since their childhoods, each of them seems to be effectively familyless. Dignan's family is mentioned only once in the film, when he protests "You know there's nothing to steal from my mom and Craig." His desperate attachment to the landscaping job he briefly held and his nearly all-consuming desire to be readmitted into the operation is explicitly explained by the owner of that outfit as a bid for some measure of belonging in his life, his desire not to be "a man alone." Anthony, though he does not lack money, seems equally adrift. Having checked himself out of the luxury mental health retreat where he is living at the film's opening, he returns to his childhood home only for the purposes of burgling it with Dignan. Otherwise, he stays conspicuously away—meeting secretively with his younger sister at her school in order to return his mother's mistakenly purloined earrings and flatly refusing his sister's entreaties to simply come back home. His stubborn claim that "I can't come home. I'm an adult" can seem like prideful postadolescent posturing, but in the wider context of the film it also points to some degree of estrangement between Anthony and his parents. Someone was paying for that posh sanitarium stay (and Anthony himself seems to have no visible means to do so), but whatever financial support may or may not continue to exist does not at any point in the film yield actual contact or connection between parents and child, not even so much as a telephone call. At one point in the story, in fact, Anthony writes to his sister to inform her that he is living with Bob in *his* childhood home and makes no mention of ever returning to his own. (An earlier version of the screenplay includes an incident in which Anthony explains to Dignan at the end of the film that he has now moved into a sailboat parked in Bob's backyard.) It is a telling choice of residence, for there is no doubt about the estrangement between Bob and his family; the only difference is that Bob's parents have essentially vacated the family homestead. Bob hasn't seen his jet-setting mother and father in months—at one point he reports "Last I heard they were in Singapore"—and he lives in fear of his unchecked older brother, who beats him mercilessly at the slightest provocation even though the two are both technically adults. Rather than an instance of aged parents entrusting their adult children to watch over the family home, the dynamics of Bob's home life more closely resemble what one might expect to unfold if the parents had simply left their adolescent children entirely alone.

As in so many Anderson films, the breakdown of basic family structures leaves the line between childhood and adulthood remarkably thin for the three central characters, such that the two life stages seem almost to bleed into one another. Yet among the sizable list of Anderson characters who wander through their adulthoods in a kind of prolonged or stunted adolescence—a tally that includes all three adult Tenenbaum children and even the aged Captain Zissou himself—the heroes of *Bottle Rocket* present an unusually dark variation on the type: not so much quirky and melancholic as sad, disaffected, and potentially dangerous. These are characters who seem to have at one point known, through experience or by proxy, the safety and order that a caring family can bring—an emotional state embodied in the carefully arranged collections of the film's opening burglary, the coin collection and toy soldier collection of Anthony's childhood being the earliest examples of Anderson's visual interest in the topos of the collection and of its thematic place within his narratives. But something undefined has gone wrong somewhere along the way, leaving these boy-men alone (Dignan), estranged (Anthony), or outright abandoned (Bob). To say they have become dangerous in their joint isolation is not to overlook the fundamental silliness of their feeble attempt at gangsterism and the absurd targets at which it is myopically directed: Anthony's childhood home and a local strip-mall bookstore chain (this still being the era when Barnes and Noble prospered). And certainly these three must be among the most polite marauders in moviedom, following a gruff demand that all their captives "sit tight" with an eager "Okay, thank you so much." Regardless, there always is something menacing in waving a gun in people's faces to get what you want. Just because a child is acting out only to get attention does not mean that nobody will get hurt; in fact, it's usually just the opposite.

Of course, attention proves harder to come by than Dignan and his associates would like. "We're fugitives," Dignan joyously declares after they pull off the bookstore heist. He insists that the group look for a "little place to lie low while the heat cools down" and even wants them to change their appearance so that they can avoid "some trooper recognizing us and throwing us in jail." But this is a game of hide and seek in which no one is bothering to do the seeking, neither law enforcement nor, pointedly, any friends or relatives of these three would-be desperados. If they had wanted to conceive a plan designed specifically to prove just how alone and unwanted they actually were, they could not have done any better. Insofar as the boys' microsyndicate was conceived, like any gang, as a kind of surrogate family, those surrogate relations begin very quickly to break down in the face of the deafening indifference of the wider world to their exploits. As Orgeron notes, Dignan and company originally plan their criminal escapades around Bob's dining room table, filling out the traditional positions of mother, father, and child that have been vacated by the boys' actual relations (50). But their new quasi-family shows no more staying power than the original ones it was meant to replace. Anthony, who believes he has fallen in love with one of the housekeepers in the motel where they have sequestered themselves, very quickly loses interest in his criminal compatriots—at one point literally getting up and running away from Dignan in the diner where they have gone to plan their next move so that he can spend more time with the housekeeper Inez (Lumi Cavazos). Bob responds to the threesome's flailing mission to get noticed by rediscovering the value of kinship bonds, racing home to help the same abusive brother he previously wanted to escape when he discovers *he* has actually been the one to attract the attention of the police and has been arrested in connection to the marijuana plants that Bob was trying to grow in the backyard. The alternate family structure into which the boys tried to collect themselves when no one else would have them, it turns out, was not any more unified than the equally parentless family of the Whitman brothers in *The Darjeeling Limited*, a unit that showed the same propensity for fracturing. Though they might arrange themselves unwittingly as mother, father, and son at Bob's dining table, the *Bottle Rocket* gang cannot escape the orphanness of their circumstance, cannot compensate for the actual absence of parental figures.

That is, until Dignan somewhat miraculously produces the surrogate parent he has claimed to be seeking all along, as elusive and mythical as Zissou's jaguar shark. From his earliest appearances in the film, Dignan has rattled on to Anthony about the great Mr. Henry, in whose gang he claims to have briefly been a member. The tale seems to be pure delusion—Dignan being the same character who at one point produced a seventy-five-year plan for the group's criminal operation, from inception to retirement, carefully written out in magic marker. Looking at the crumpled snapshot of the gang that Dignan carries with him like a talisman, Bob points out to Anthony that it's just a photo of the landscaping crew Dignan once worked for (fig. 18). Yet in a development straight out of Max Fischer's imagination, it turns out that Dignan was telling the truth all along—the landscaping crew was a front for Mr. Henry's criminal enterprise, and having learned of the boys' bookstore break-in, this small-time crime boss has invited the three into his gang. Like the pirate interlude in *The Life Aquatic*, the encounter with Mr. Henry and his criminal associates has something of the quality of a dream and seems to stand apart from the rest of the film. Living together in an enormous loft snatched from some child's imagined version of a criminal's hideout,

Mr. Henry and his crew seem to pass their time mostly playing pranks on one another and practicing karate in their underwear like wanton boys left without supervision. They still seem like they could simply be figments of Dignan's fevered imagination even as they enter the movie's narrative and interact with the other characters. But, like the pirates, their effect is real enough. The promise of an actual criminal gang life like that offered by Mr. Henry—which is in effect the promise of a surrogate family on a much larger scale than the boys could create on their own—is enough to bring the three back together and recommit them to the life of crime they had abandoned. In addition to its greater size and scope, the surrogate family offered by Mr. Henry has one other very important advantage: a surrogate parent. In fact, Mr. Henry may actually be one of the most caring and attentive father figures in Anderson's filmography, which admittedly is a fairly limited distinction. Like Royal and Zissou after him, Mr. Henry takes it upon himself to police the boundaries of the family over which he presides and to govern the adoption of new members. Only after Dignan has convinced him of his criminal bona fides does Mr. Henry allow the young acolyte and his friends entry into the group, subjecting them to a kind of adolescent initiation ritual by dropping water on them from the roof of his warehouse building before letting them into the hideout. Yet once they are admitted into the group, the boys experience none of the stifling identity enforcement

Figure 18. Dignan's faux-family portrait

that both Royal and Zissou attempt to maintain. Mr. Henry's enterprise is defined from the start by the we-centricity that other Anderson outfits achieve only over time. Multiracial, multiethnic, and multigenerational, Mr. Henry's gang is a playful and freeform venture wherein he has supposedly gathered the best of the best of the criminal underworld, a collective governed by an idea of likeness so fine that it takes Mr. Henry to discern the kernel of similarity binding together a septuagenarian South Asian safe-cracker and a boyish kid from the suburbs with only the most limited criminal experience. Mr. Henry seems to have the eye of the most expert collector, one whose highly eclectic assortment of criminal misfits is supposed to stand as manifest proof of his unerring discernment.

And it's also a complete lie. As Dignan, Anthony, and Bob discover only too late, Mr. Henry does have a real criminal syndicate, but it's not the fantasy one into which they have been inducted. Sending the boys off on a special mission to rob the Hinckley Cold Storage facility equipped with everything from matching jumpsuits to special smoke bombs, Mr. Henry has his real criminal associates do their dirty work with only dollies and a moving truck—robbing Bob's family home of every last costly item inside while Bob and the others are away performing the dummy heist. Whether or not the joyous eclecticism of Mr. Henry's front-gang had any basis in reality, the dour heavies who pull off the real burglary certainly seem more in keeping with the kind of top-down, humorless operation one might expect from an actual criminal leader. The kind of open and accepting alternate-family construction premised on a logic of likeness and an ethos of common but uncoercive similarity—that is, the very goal to which so many Anderson characters and collectives actually aspire—is here shown to be just another boyish dream and a potentially dangerous fantasy. Dignan certainly suffers for it. When the cold storage heist goes bust, Dignan is the only one of the three central friends to be caught, and he is consigned for believing in his fantasies to a kind of special filmic prison—the Wasco State Penitentiary, the one named for Anderson's production designers. The comingled dreams of adventure and belonging that are such a powerful motivating force for all Anderson's familyless boy-men, Zissou and Max Fischer alike, here lead Dignan to the point of self-destruction, a life of endless monotony and enforced social isolation wherein his only possible escape is imaginary.

But before his moment of incarceration, Dignan is at least afforded a fleeting moment of grace. His capture immanent, he makes a final stand of sorts and defiantly declares, "They'll never catch me, man. 'Cause I'm fucking innocent." It's a baldly illogical statement by just about any possible measure: Dignan is quite obviously guilty and is in fact still standing on the grounds of the facility he was just trying to rob, gun in hand; he most certainly is about to be caught by the police who are already on their way; and the two characteristics, being caught and being innocent, really have no cause-and-effect relationship whatsoever—even if he were innocent, it would not make him any less likely to get caught. On its surface, the statement is pure nonsense. It also is among the most profound sentiments in Anderson's body of films, what Scorsese calls in his assessment of *Bottle Rocket* a "transcendent moment." Dignan is innocence incarnate, a grown man who still writes in spiral-bound notebooks in magic marker and believes with all his heart there is a family of some kind or another waiting for him, some kind of special group that he can join if he just tries hard enough to find it or to create it. Even in his prison uniform at the end of the film, he remains undefeated, uncaught. Neither prison nor the knowledge of Mr. Henry's betrayal has done anything to squelch his boyishness. "We did it, though, didn't we?" he asks Anthony and Bob when they come to visit him in prison, still convinced in the success of their failed enterprise. For better or for worse, his is a potentially eternal innocence, eternal because the circumstances that created it and to which it is a defensive response may never in fact be resolved. Maybe, the film seems to posit, if you never manage to find your family, you never have to actually grow up.

Shelf 3: Anderson's Matched Pairs

Moonrise Kingdom (2012) For all its differences from the other films in the Anderson canon, *Bottle Rocket* effectively encapsulates in two bookended quotations the controlling thematic dynamics of much of the director's filmmaking. Between Anthony's statement near the opening of the film explaining "I can't come home. I'm an adult" and Dignan's statement near the end proclaiming "They'll never catch me, man. 'Cause I'm fucking innocent" lies the central emotional and thematic struggle of Anderson's films: isolated and estranged by familial breakdown, Anderson's protagonists are at once pushed into a world of adult dislocation even while they are pulled backward by the appeal of childhood innocence. Anderson's characters are in thrall to the emotional appeal of the collection and its promise that from the disordered pieces of the world new orders can be created and a sense of belonging can be furtively retrieved. From *Bottle Rocket* through *Fantastic Mr. Fox*, the family, the collection, and the collective stand intertwined. In the director's two most recent works, however, *Moonrise Kingdom* and *The Grand Budapest Hotel*, a new direction emerges in relation to these themes. Anderson's protagonists remain as isolated as ever, arguably more so: the families from which they come are not just broken but obliterated, rendered utterly irretrievable. The institutions meant to take the place of those families are either stifling or actively dangerous, offering only the worst version of the kind of collectivity that so many Anderson characters seek. In many ways, these films present an extreme case of the typical Anderson predicament, and the responses to it prove equally extreme. Rather than try to restore or recreate the lost or broken family, Anderson's new protagonists utterly reject it as an institution or an ideal. With no possibility of retrieving the family, Anderson's newest heroes have likewise abandoned the promise of the collective—though not of the collection itself. Rather, they have refined the demands of the collection and reduced its expansive imperative down to its absolute simplest state: the matched pair. Their quest is analogous to that which Benjamin describes in *The Arcades Project* as the collector who "is shown a panel of an altar screen [and] remembers in what church, museum, and private collection the other panels are dispersed [until] . . . he finally succeeds, by following the catalogs of art sales or frequenting antique shops, in finding the mate to the object he possesses and thereby completing the pair" (211). The collection efforts of these characters likewise require only one acquisition to reach completion, but it must be the perfect one. The collectivity they build is the collectivity of two; the we-centricity they seek is plural but not multiple. That pairing may be romantic, as in the childhood love affair of *Moonrise Kingdom*, or it may be professional, as in the central mentorship of *The Grand Budapest Hotel*. Either way, though, it is designed as a bulwark: a structure simple enough to immediately provide the sense of belonging that all Anderson characters seek and yet strong enough to withstand the inevitable onslaughts it must face, whether the literal storms that descend on the characters in *Moonrise* or the geopolitical tempests that beset *Budapest*. The group enterprise explored in Anderson's earlier films has always been a difficult and largely unstable one, as prone to catastrophic failure within his narratives as it is to a limited and always qualified success. The shift from the group to the pair is a response to these difficulties in extremis and a reduction of the ethos of collecting down to its essence. The logic of likeness still pervades Anderson's thematics, but it is no longer the end goal of a willed act of collective construction but rather the object of a kind of personal quest—one that begins not in a pining for the lost innocence of family life but in its uncompromised rejection as a viable ideal.

Of course, no character in Anderson's body of films has more cause to reject the institution of the family than Sam Shakusky (Jared Gilman) in *Moonrise Kingdom*. Unique among Anderson's characters up to this point, Sam is an unadopted orphan, a twelve-year-old child whose parents passed away "a number of years ago" in the words of his latest caretaker. Sam's familial trauma is arguably the greatest of any Anderson character so far, but for all the emotional turmoil he has undoubtedly gone through, Sam has no illusions about the problematic enterprise of constructing an alternate family structure to take the place of that which was lost. He has spent the better part of his childhood as a ward of the state living in a series of foster homes, none of which has led to an adoption and some of which have barely attempted to recreate the basic structures of family life at all. His most recent residence is in a group home that houses seven boys in total and where the children sleep in dormitory-style rooms and spend their days performing menial chores. Though the character of Mr. Billingsley (Larry Pine) refers to himself and his wife as Sam's "foster parents," there seems to be very little parenting at all in this arrangement. Sam may be cheerful in describing the foster home, saying to Suzy (Kara Hayward) "I feel like I'm in a family now. Not like yours, but similar to one." But his acceptance of his circumstances runs only so deep, and he is expelled from the home early in the film for starting fires in his sleep. His next stop within the imagined foster care system of the film's universe makes no claims to recreating any aspect of familial life at all. It is something called "Juvenile Refuge," which resembles an orphanage but involves "a psychological evaluation to determine whether or not the boy's a candidate for institutional treatment or electroshock therapy."

Whereas so many Anderson characters attempt to compensate for the breakdown of familial structures by trying to force their reengagement or to craft some functional replacement, Sam's life has been lived in and through the failure of such efforts. So impersonal is the foster care system in which he has grown up that the civil servant in charge of his transmission from one foster family arrangement to another does not ever use (or, more chillingly, may not even have) an actual name; she is referred to metonymically as "Social Services" (Tilda Swinton) throughout the film and introduces herself as such. The extrafamilial institutions in which Sam is simultaneously enrolled hardly offer any greater sense of community or belonging. Having spent at least two summers as a Khaki Scout, Sam remains, by the scoutmaster's account, "the least popular scout in the troop, by a significant margin." He is adept at scouting work and interested in it (in fact, Scoutmaster Ward [Edward Norton] praises profusely the campsite Sam has made at his getaway beachhead), but this ability buys him neither friends nor mentors. The Khaki Scouts represent the kind of uniformed institution that typically connotes an ethos of stultifying sameness within Anderson's films rather than one of likeness and accepted eccentricity. Though Scoutmaster Ward's outpost seems more permissive than most, and the scouts are involved in any number of bizarre self-directed projects that Ward only cursorily inspects, the main Khaki Scout camp depicted later in the film is almost crypto-fascist in the uniformity of its scouts' appearances and comportment and the precision of its scout formations. Even in Ward's more open scouting environment, Sam stands out more than can be accepted. Or, more specifically, his lack of collective attachment in one arena all but precludes his acceptance in any other: "He's emotionally disturbed because his family died," his fellow Khaki Scouts announce by way of explaining their animosity toward him. Cast outside the normative bonds of family life, Sam is rendered in the eyes of those around him essentially unassimilable. His only available option, it seems to him, is to simply escape those structures into which he has been placed and of which he has never become a part. "Listen to some reason: I don't like you. You don't like me. Why don't you stupid idiots just let us disappear?" Sam says to the scouts who are tracking him.

Sam's partner in this escape mission is a character who, on the surface, could not seem more different in circumstance from this troubled orphan. Suzy Bishop lives in a beautiful, rambling New England home with three brothers and two parents. Not counting the animated family of *Fantastic Mr. Fox*, hers is actually the only stable two-parent home depicted in all of Anderson's films; every other family in his body of work has been touched in some way by death or by divorce. But neither the family's material comfort nor its apparent completeness can make Suzy feel as though she belongs in it. Prone to lashing out verbally at her parents and to lashing out violently at her school peers, Suzy has been labeled by her family as a "very troubled child," judging by the title of the manual *Coping with the Very Troubled Child* that she discovers among her parents' belongings. It might be more accurate, however, to say of Suzy that she is a very perceptive child in a very troubled household.

Though it holds the unique distinction of having held together so far, the Bishop family also is distinguished by being among the most unloving in Anderson's body of films. Mr. Bishop (Bill Murray) is a remarkably depressive and distant father whose emotional desperation borders on the suicidal. He actively wishes for his own annihilation, remarking to his wife at one point "I hope the roof flies off, and I get sucked up into space. You'll be better off without me." Mrs. Bishop's (Frances McDormand's) response has been to seek some measure of comfort and companionship outside the marriage: She is engaged in an affair with the community's sole police officer and is so inexpert or uncaring in her elopements that she meets her lover close enough to the house for Suzy to watch their liaisons through binoculars. Against this troubled pairing, Suzy's three brothers have formed a kind of emotional phalanx. Almost always pictured together engaged in shared activities, they seem to have retreated into a hermetically sealed version of childhood that keeps them emotionally protected against their actual family life. It is a dynamic that reaches a particularly disturbing level of intensity in the brief scene where Mr. Bishop, shirtless, with a bottle of red wine and a glass in one hand and an ax in the other, stands behind the three boys playing a board game together and announces, in full volume, that he is "going to find a tree to chop down," channeling what seem to be Jack-Nicholson-in-*The-Shining* levels of anger and resentment at his family into an unmotivated attack on the family homestead (fig. 19). Caught between her parents' emotional battles on the one hand and her brothers' emotional retreat on the other, Suzy is effectively orphaned inside

Figure 19. Fun and games in *Moonrise Kingdom* |

her own family and stands aligned with neither parents nor siblings. By way of emphasis, Anderson opens *Moonrise Kingdom* with one of his trademark Ophüls-style pans through a cutaway of the Bishop household set to the music of Benjamin Britten's *Young Person's Guide to the Orchestra*. Emblematic of a certain kind of cultivated childhood, Britten's piece also is a schematic explanation of an orchestral system in which every instrument has a defined place among others of its kind. Neither Sam nor Suzy has any such place or any such kind—at least, not until they discover each other.

That discovery will take place under the sign of another of Britten's orchestral works designed in part for children, one that plays a particularly prominent narrative and thematic role in Anderson's film: the opera *Noye's Fludde*. An operatic rendition of the story of Noah's Ark designed specifically for amateur performance by churches and community organizations, Britten's folk opera was meant to enable laypersons and nonprofessionals to act out the great biblical story of collection and escape in their own communities. It is a mission that Sam and Suzy take particularly to heart. The story of Noah's Ark is one of the preeminent legends of collection-as-traumatic-recovery: after the great destruction of the flood, the special collection of animals that Noah has carefully amassed on his ark will repopulate the world, bringing both order and life to the desolated landscape. Indeed, the story of the ark was one of

Benjamin's favorite metaphors for describing both his own collector's impulse and his own collected works, writing in an inscription in one of his books given to a friend "may you . . . find a chamber in this ark—which I built when the Fascist flood was starting to rise—for the memories of your youth" (qtd. in Eiland 538). But if Noah's Ark presents the story of collection set against a rising tide of destruction, it also is the story of a collection of a very particular kind: a collection by way of matched pairs, "of beastes uncleane towe and towe" (Pollard 12), in the words of the medieval play text that Britten set to music. It is here, under the auspices of this tale of the restorative power of collection, that Sam and Suzy discover that they themselves can in fact form such a matched pair, that they may be the same "towe and towe" prized so highly in the opera. "What kind of bird are you?" Sam asks Suzy pointedly after sneaking backstage into her dressing room during the show. Another girl begins to answer Sam's query by explaining which bird each of the assembled girls represents, but Sam is not interested in general taxonomies. "No, I said what kind of bird are *you*" he asks Suzy again, pointing his finger directly at her. Something in Suzy's person or performance has led Sam to believe that they two might form a pair when neither has ever found a partner of any kind before. Noah must take from the earth pairs of animals, "iche one in his kinde" in the words of the medieval lyrics of Britten's opera, and it may be that Sam and Suzy, who both always felt so alone themselves, form two of their own "kinde" (Pollard 14).

Lest there be any doubt about the rightness of this pairing or any attempt to dismiss these children's coupling as just a kind of childhood infatuation, Anderson's camera renders the eventual union of Sam and Suzy a year later in the wilds of New Penzance Island as an almost cosmological event, a pairing worthy of divine sanctioning in the manner of Noah's collection. During the pair's rendezvous in an idyllic high-grassed meadow that seems to have been lifted straight out of an Andrew Wyeth painting, Anderson's planimetric frame transforms the natural landscape into a realm of pure Cartesian order. Prominently placing the horizon line across the bottom quarter of the frame with a windmill strategically stationed precisely at its center, Anderson positions Sam and Suzy first in a tableau of perfect symmetry and then in a series of progressively constructed symmetries, each character's individual medium shot equally balancing the other's frame until at last they meet together at

Figure 20. Sam and Suzy's impossible
rendezvous, part 1

the middle. Yet while the overwhelming symmetry of this sequence is
frequently noted, what is less commonly observed is the fact that the
individual series of balanced shots leading up to the rendezvous in the
middle creates a visually impossible sequence. Diegetically, Sam and
Suzy are calling out to each other from across the field, as seen in the
establishing long shot (fig. 20). Visually, they are each standing no more
than a few feet from another in their respective medium shots, as judged
from their sudden proximity to the central windmill, which is used to
establish balance in their individual frames (figs. 21, 22). For a director
as visually meticulous as Anderson, this quite obvious visual continuity
error is no mere accident. Like the obvious and intentional continuity
errors in Chaplin's famous shot/reverse shot sequence at the end of *City
Lights*, Anderson is here breaking the diegesis of his constructed world
on purpose. Sam and Suzy's reunion has literally broken the rules of the
existing world around them, not by unleashing chaos but by enforcing a
too-perfect order. It is as though their meeting has set this broken world
too much aright and enforced a kind of impossible symmetry that is not
usually allowed. This idea of a too-perfect order being brought into the
world is visually echoed again when the two finally set up camp at the
Mile 3.25 Tidal Inlet after a visually jagged journey through the wilderness—one of only a few instances of handheld camerawork in Anderson's
body of films. Shaped into a nearly perfect horseshoe, the beachhead

Figure 21. Sam and Suzy's impossible
rendezvous, part 2

Figure 22. Sam and Suzy's impossible
rendezvous, part 3

where Sam and Suzy declare their independence from the wider world
is a place not just of sanctuary but of impeccable order and balance, an
order that seems to visually emanate from their very pairing. Setting
their camp at the base of the horseshoe, the two lay claim to the space
by running up opposite sides of the shoreline until they reach each tip
of the horseshoe shore. "This is our land!" they declare before jumping

simultaneously into the water. The imposition of Anderson's trademark visual symmetry, which is usually confined to urban and interior spaces, onto the undeveloped landscape of New England's famously ragged coastline confers on the pair a rare power of visual configuration, as if they were able to remake the world itself according to their newfound sense of inner balance. This is the dream of so many Anderson characters—to achieve an inner sense of belonging through affiliation with some outside person or persons and to have that sense of order broadcast over the world itself; here it is made manifest in the most literal of ways for arguably the first time in Anderson's body of films, a small corner of the world briefly made perfect through interpersonal communion.

Were Sam and Suzy adults who were alone in the world when they found each other, like so many other Anderson characters before them, then perhaps this idyll would never need to end; at least it could stand a chance of coming to a close on their own terms. But Sam and Suzy's claims to adulthood are a pretense, one manifest not only in their stolen independence but also in the unearned position of knowledgeability they often take with one another or in the weary and disaffected tone each of them frequently strikes. Their willfully premature maturity forms a kind of direct inversion and counterpoint to the willfully prolonged adolescence or childishness of so many other Anderson characters. Both stances are a cover and an attempt to escape from painful conditions. But alone among Anderson's various attempted world creators, Sam and Suzy are actually pursued, passionately so. Typically, Anderson's families and creative approximations thereof are remarkable mostly for the degree to which they are unnoticed and forgotten by the wider world—witness the characters in *Bottle Rocket* languishing unpursued in their motel; the degree to which "virtually all memory" of the once-great Tenenbaums "had been erased"; the fact that Zissou's entire remaining social network can fit with him in one little submarine at the film's end; or the total global isolation of the Whitman brothers traveling alone through India. But unlike these predecessors, Sam and Suzy's creation of a world apart is not a response to their own literal displacement in the world; rather, it is a response to an acute sense of displacement experienced inside the structures in which they are supposed to feel belonging. Put another way, the trauma from which they are running is not that of dispersion per se but of the institutions and groups into which they have been forcibly assigned as a sanctioned means of corralling or forestalling such dispersion—the unloving foster families into which Sam has been placed in response to the trauma of his parents' death or the deeply unhealthy family environment that Suzy is not allowed to critique or to leave despite the anger and desperation it clearly creates in her. Sam and Suzy both feel misplaced in the world in the most literal sense, not forgotten but rather miscollected or misassigned. But their attempt to remedy this misplacement, while intended as a self-directed emotional salve, is also inevitably a social critique—one that leaves a wound in the social structures left behind as gaping and unmistakable as the perfectly round hole that Sam cuts out of the fabric of his tent when he first makes his break.

In a world that has decided it already knows best how to contain their trauma, Sam and Suzy's joint decision to opt out and administer their own relief is an inadmissible act of independence, one that leaves an unacceptable level of wreckage in their wake—a prominent and prosperous family missing a member and a government welfare service missing a charge. The ferocity with which these two children are pursued is in itself a testament to the desperation of the pursuers' efforts to close the punctum that the children have opened. This ferocity is manifest most directly in Sam's Khaki Scout peers, who arm themselves with any manner of elaborate and potentially lethal homemade weapons to aid in their pursuit. Scoutmaster Ward claims that their mission is merely to "to *find* him, not to *hurt* him," but he has no answer to the scouts' astute question of "What if he resists? . . . Are we allowed to use force on him?" The unspoken answer, whether Ward is willing to admit it or not, is that they must force him, the young scouts being just a little too explicit in their methods. But there is only a difference of degree, not of kind, in the manner in which Mr. Bishop eventually acts when the young escapees are discovered in their hideaway. Grunting like an animal and tearing their small tent from the ground like some giant ogre of mythology, Suzy's father forcibly grabs his daughter and physically brings her to the boat that will carry them back to civilization. There is no accommodation to the challenge Sam and Suzy's escape presented, only a forcible restoration of old conditions. Suzy is returned to the family she thought enough to run away from, screaming "I hate you" almost as soon as she returns home; Sam is reported to Social Services and prepared for a transfer to Juvenile Refuge.

The horror of these restored conditions—what we might call the enforced trauma of the normal—is what eventually saves Sam and Suzy and prompts their second escape in the film. There is nothing especially uncommon about the sentences that Sam and Suzy are given—she to her family and he to the next stage of the foster care system. But the prospective violence of these situations, emotional for Suzy and possibly physical for Sam in the electroshock treatments that may be part of life in his supposed refuge, are enough to shift the loyalties of Sam's Khaki Scout compatriots, who also were the first to recognize the violence inherent in the original pursuit. "He's a fellow Khaki Scout, and he needs our help. . . . So part of his brain doesn't get removed out of him," one of them declares during a secret meeting, and they resolve to help the two lovers escape again once and for all. Theirs is not an entirely selfless act. They do not, for instance, offer to befriend and to accept the formal social outcast and beg of their superiors that he remain a part of their organization and stay on their island, near them and near Suzy; they do not open any space in their own social unit for him or try to find a point of likeness with him, reiterating several times even as they decide to help him that "he's emotionally disturbed" because of his status as "a disadvantaged orphan." Instead of attempting to offer camaraderie, they try to simply effect together a more complete version of the total social escape that Sam and Suzy first attempted alone. Where Sam and Suzy first enacted a tentative and largely presexual courtship, the scouts will offer a ceremony of marriage presided over by the cousin of one of the scouts, an older "Falcon Scout" who is also "a civil-law scrivener . . . authorized to declare births, deaths, and marriages." Where Sam and Suzy first attempted a flight to the wilderness, the scouts will offer a flight from the very land borders of society itself—a life lived out upon a "cold-water crabber." "The skipper owes me an I.O.U." says the scrivener. "We'll see if he can take you on as a claw cracker. It won't be an easy life, but it's better than shock therapy." Where Sam left a gaping hole in the wall of his tent as an unmistakable trace of his disappearance, the scouts will leave papier-mâché dummies to cover their tracks, trying to conceal as long as possible the wounds they are reinflicting through this second departure. There is no acceptance of difference in this offer, just a promise of a more complete expulsion.

Yet the Khaki Scouts' involvement in Sam and Suzy's second escape is pivotal in eventually brokering a solution to the problem of the pair's continual attempts at a unilateral withdrawal from society. The question implicitly posed by the scouts in their decision to reengage with the escapees and assist them in their mission is essentially the same as the one that they posed directly to Scoutmaster Ward: What if he resists? Are we allowed to use force on him? Meaning, to what extent and in what manner are the forces of social order willing to impose their preordained arrangements—the institutions of family and its socially sanctioned approximations in the foster care system—upon those who don't consent and who want to reposition themselves, who want to determine their own proper place and discover their own matched pairs? It is this question that is made visually manifest when toward the climax of the film Captain Sharp (Bruce Willis), once charged with pursuing and capturing the two runaways, picks up one of the homemade weapons previously used by the Khaki Scouts in their pursuit of Sam and Suzy and holds it in defense of the children that he was formerly pursuing. Here Sharp acknowledges the implicit violence that always backs up attempts at social enforcement but aligns himself with the scouts in resolving to use the violence entrusted in him to a different end. The scout's simple query has ultimately exposed a fundamental fissure point, an unresolved question of for whose benefit the enforced social arrangements that Sam and Suzy so vehemently protest actually exist. On this issue, the institutional forces of social order manifested in the film are turned suddenly against one another. The Troop 55 Khaki Scouts finds themselves opposed to the rest of the Khaki Scout organization in trying to help Sam and Suzy navigate through the main scout headquarters at Fort Lebanon while being relentlessly pursued. Social Services and Captain Ward soon find themselves directly at odds, vehemently issuing citations against one another for different violations of the social order and its accompanying ideological edifice. "I'm citing you for gross misconduct! You are hereby summoned to appear before the board of . . ." Social Services shouts at the policeman. "I'm writing you up *back!*" he interrupts. "Be notified that you stand accused of the mistreatment and improper . . ."

In the end, though, it is not entirely clear that Sam and Suzy's pairing is fundamentally a social question at all, despite its unavoidable social ramifications. Much of Anderson's film suggests the issue is ultimately spiritual, even cosmological. Hence the return to St. Jack's Church, site of the *Noye's Fludde* performance at which Sam and Suzy first met one year earlier, this time in the context of a real-world flood that reaches nearly biblical proportions, breaking down dams and flooding Fort Lebanon before nearly submersing the whole of the surrounding town. The storm, in the words of Anderson's omniscient narrator, "was considered by the U.S. Department of Inclement Weather to be the region's most destructive meteorological event of the second half of the twentieth century." The storm offers to Anderson's characters a kind of smaller-scale reenactment of the story of *Noye's Fludde* not as performance but as lived reality, presenting them directly with the question of what pairs they will allow or disallow, whether they themselves will fulfill the opera's divine mandate to protect "iche one in his kinde." Hiding in plain sight under animal masks that conceal their faces, Sam and Suzy have declared themselves to be a matched pair, animals of the same species. And if they will not be allowed to live together in peace, then they are willing to suffer extinction. The prospect of a double suicide by twelve-year-old children comes uncomfortably close to fruition in the film's climactic moment, one of those instances where the depth of the darkness inherent in much of Anderson's subject matter far exceeds easy dismissals of his work as being primarily an exercise in style. "If it's too shallow, we'll break our necks" Suzy openly admits when she suggests she and Sam jump into the water below. "Just in case this is a suicide," Sam says, "thank you for marrying me." Whether or not the pairing will be acceptable to the adults tasked with their supervision and well-being, Sam and Suzy are convinced of the rightness and inescapability of their union. There is no world in which they will not live as the pair that they have made, even if that means there is no world.

What saves Sam and Suzy—and the film—from utter darkness and destruction is a single humane act, perhaps the only one performed by an adult in the entire story: Captain Sharp offers to become Sam's foster parent, allowing for a path to a final compromised solution. Sam and Suzy will not run away and will not prematurely marry (their Khaki Scout marriage holds no legal standing in the end) but neither will they be forever separated. Suzy will return to her family, but she will no longer be so alone. Sam will return to foster care, but not to the Juvenile

Refuge held in so much dread. The film's resolution is not exactly what one would call a happy ending, and many of the narrative problems introduced early in the film remain unresolved. Captain Sharp's gesture of foster parentage is heartfelt, but at the same time he does not at any point offer to actually adopt Sam. Their relationship remains contingent, and the fact that Sharp and Sam begin to dress alike at the very end of the film should raise alarms within Anderson's filmic world. Their shared attire is reminiscent of Chas's relationship with Ari and Uzi in *The Royal Tenenbaums* or Zissou's exercises of parental authority in *The Life Aquatic*, and one wonders what emotional issues might be being worked out through this sudden semiparentage by the figure Suzy once described as "that sad, dumb policeman." Likewise, we do not know whether Sharp and Mrs. Bishop ever ceased their clandestine affair (now rendered quasi-incestuous by the pseudo-marriage of their respective children) or for that matter how close to imploding the Bishop family still is. We do not even know whether Sam and Suzy are actually allowed to see each other any longer—though if they are not, Suzy's brothers are at least willing to countenance his visits. The film ends with Sam sneaking out the window of Suzy's home when she and her brothers are called down to dinner, announcing that he will be back tomorrow. Whether this is just a childish performance of secrecy or the result of an actual prohibition against Sam by Suzy's parents is unknowable. In one sense, at least, though, it doesn't much matter either way. In the film's final moments, Sam is supposedly painting a portrait of Suzy, as he has done at earlier points in the story. But a pan to his canvas in the film's closing moments reveals that while looking at her he was actually painting a landscape of the beach they once inhabited together, now since "erased from the map" by the great storm. For Sam, within Suzy's person is always carried the vision of that place and that moment, the knowledge and the memory of their relationship in its most perfect instance. Their connection no longer requires any special place or special sanctioning, no particular monument or marker, no special privileges. The collection they have unilaterally formed against the contexts into which they were born or placed, their special status as a special matched pair, cannot be breached or taken away because it exists internally; it has become a state of mind and a state of being, a condition for which so many figures in Anderson's films have fleetingly reached. The resolution to which Sam and Suzy come is arguably the most mature conclusion reached by any of Anderson's characters.

The Grand Budapest Hotel (2014)   If *Moonrise Kingdom* comes to a resolution in a special confluence of personage and place, that same dynamic is present from the outset of *The Grand Budapest Hotel*. Presented in a series of nested stories, first of an author who comes to define the spirit of his nation, then of a wealthy businessman met by that author who defines for him the faded but once-glorious hotel in which he is staying, and then of the great hotel concierge known by that businessman who was once synonymous with the place itself, *Budapest* takes as one of its starting premises the idea that people and places can fade into one another and become inseparable. To fall in love with a person may be to fall in love with the places that define that person, the nation that contains those places, even the era that defined that nation. In this way, *Budapest* is, like *Moonrise Kingdom*, another love story, though of a qualitatively different kind. Its central affair is not between two young romantics but between two men in love with the same place and the same time, in thrall to an idea of historical and cultural belonging that they find ultimately to be best expressed through one another. Set visually and thematically amid some of Anderson's most expansive and expensive diegetic collections—from the world-class private art collection of the Family Desgoffe-und-Taxis to the imperial collections of the Kunstmuseum—*Budapest* is nonetheless a film that, like *Moonrise*, focuses acutely on the power of the matched pair. Here, two of Anderson's most unlikely potential matches—a refined and dandyish hotel concierge and the hard-nosed but wide-eyed refugee who becomes his protégé—discover through their shared love for a grand but fading institution of middle European culture and cultivation a fundamental likeness in each other. Bereft of family but with access to any number of potential avenues for alternative constructions of collectivity and group identity, mentor and mentee eschew such larger groupings for the one pairing that gives them both meaning, their special professional interchange being among the most complete interpenetrations of self and other in Anderson's body of work.

That Anderson's two protagonists should seek identification and solace only in one another should perhaps come as no surprise when one considers the greater dynamics of the world that they inhabit. If the collective groupings in the universe of *Moonrise Kingdom* have become deeply dysfunctional, as tempestuous as the Bishop family homestead or as depersonalizing as the Khaki Scout's main base at Fort Lebanon, in the world of *The Grand Budapest Hotel* such collectives have become downright dangerous. Here, the main family of Anderson's narrative, the extensive Family Desgoffe-und-Taxis, is something closer to a cartel than a kinship unit, complete with murderous hired goons. Likewise, the depersonalization of the Khaki Scouts has now evolved into the fascist thuggery of the Zubrowka military. The darker side of collectivity, which has always been part of Anderson's subtext, has now lurched to the foreground of his filmmaking. Here, the collection is not comforting but hazardous, even deadly: in fact, all of the film's many murders are prompted by a single question of transmissibility and inheritance, a dispute over the propriety of the bequest of a single painting separated from the rest of the Family Desgoffe-und-Taxis's vast art collection. Thinking back to the obsession over keeping collections intact that marked the beginning of Anderson's filmmaking—to Anthony's protests over the removal of an earring from his mother's mahogany box in *Bottle Rocket* or to his compulsive righting of the toy soldier that has come out of place on the shelf in that film's opening sequence—it is possible to recognize in *The Grand Budapest Hotel* the nightmarish extrapolation of those seemingly innocent preservationist impulses.

This new nightmarishness of the collection is literalized in *Budapest* in the film's masterfully shot chase through the fictional Kunstmuseum. It is a deeply recursive sequence, with Deputy Kovacs (Jeff Goldblum), the upright lawyer of the Desgoffe-und-Taxis family, attempting to flee from Jopling (Willem Dafoe), the sociopathic enforcer of the same grand family, when the central dispute about the breakup of the family's art collection turns violent—an escape that Kovacs effects by entering and trying to navigate the site of an even larger and more elaborate art collection, the grandest such collection in Anderson's filmography. Kovacs is successful to a point in his escape, at least at first. Up and down staircases, across art galleries, through chambers holding antique armor and Egyptian artifacts, Anderson pictures Kovacs alone and one step ahead of his pursuer, protected from the dangers of the world by a retreat into the collection. Yet Jopling is always just a short distance behind his prey, his lurking presence communicated in a series of expressionist touches apropos of Anderson's middle European setting: a flash of light across the museum lobby as he opens the door, a long shadow cast over the grand staircase, the ominous sound of his boots on the marble floor, a brief shot in silhouette at the far end of a long gallery hall. The production design of the museum tableaux is as dense and wondrous as any in Anderson's work, with its towering gallery wall whose every inch is covered in paintings and its darkened room full of individually lit suits of armor lined up like so many giant toy soldiers. The Kunstmuseum is a kind of apotheosis of the walls covered in childhood drawings and rooms full of childhood toy collections that marked the director's earlier films. Here that saturated visual terrain—what art historian Barbara Maria Stafford would call the "information-rich geography" of the collection (75)—is overcast by a lighting plot and sound design that is pure horror. Quite literally, there is no place to hide in the world of the collection anymore; the collection's special ability to fend off the encroachments of the dangerous realms outside its boundaries is now officially broken in Anderson's filmmaking. Kovacs is disfigured and murdered inside this grand museum collection and then unceremoniously stuffed into an Egyptian sarcophagus by his undeterrable pursuer. The collection, always a place of brokenness as Thomas reminds us ("Objects tend, by definition, to find their way into a collection . . . when their world is disappearing or has been destroyed," she writes [172]), has now become a place of death, which in some sense it always has been as well.

It is little wonder that in such a world Zero and Gustave would both decide to eschew the prerogatives of the wider collection and the wider collective and instead seek their perfect other only in the individual to whom they feel best matched—which is also a kind of collection, just of the most intimate kind. The search for identity through another person, the mission to discover one's own matched pair, is not an easy one and not one typically undertaken outside the bounds of romance. It represents the ultimate refinement of the collection process, a search for meaning and security born of the collector's impulse toward the arrangement and possession of like things—a possession that, as Graham writes, "can fend off the chaos of the infinite material world, the loss of memory, the passage of time and the passing of objects into oblivion" (52). Like so many of Anderson's pictures, then, *Budapest* is a film whose central search for order and arrangement begins in trauma, the loss of familial identity prompting the pursuit of alternate avenues of meaning. That original trauma, revealed slowly over the course of the film, belongs to Zero Moustafa (Tony Revolori). Zero is, after Sam Shakusky, the second orphan in Anderson's body of works, though arguably his losses even go beyond what Sam has suffered. Zero has lost not only his family but his very nation and the entire way of life he once knew. At various points in the film, Zero recounts how his "father was murdered, and the rest of my family were executed by firing squad," how he was "arrested and tortured by the rebel militia after the Desert Uprising," how his "village was burned to the ground," and how "those who managed to survive were forced to flee." That which he has lost is beyond restoration and is now entirely unrecoverable—even the country from which he came, racked by civil war, will presumably never be the same. Zero is, as his name implies, beginning entirely anew. In Gustave's summation of his interview, he stands at "Experience: Zero," "Education: Zero," and "Family: Zero." He has come looking not just for a new place of employment but for a new home, a new world even.

Yet to say that Zero has come to the nation of Zubrowka seeking refuge is in some way overstating the case as it is presented in the film: He has come specifically to the Grand Budapest Hotel, which functions as a kind of country unto itself. Set apart on a mountaintop perch overlooking the spa town of Nebelsbad, it is reachable by car or by the Colonnade Funicular: One must embark on a deliberate journey to travel there, one does not just casually stop by. The world inside the hotel is governed by its own rules and mores, the work papers issued to its foreign employees functioning effectively like passports—in both instances where Zero is stopped by the military during a rail journey, he produces the paperwork that permits him to work at the Grand Budapest while the other passengers produce the documents of their nationhood, their actual passports. Indeed, when war at last breaks out in the film, the Grand Budapest is effectively the first occupied nation, its services entirely taken over by the military of Zubrowka, who drape their flags over the façade of the hotel like a conquering army.

For all of the Grand Budapest's vaunted history, visual distinctiveness, and semi-independence from the world around it, however, its status as a grand institution of central European life rests on a remarkably thin foundation within the film: It is a status much talked about but hardly actually seen. We learn nothing, for instance, about the actual history of the hotel, about its origins or its great figures of the past. Aside from the purported fame of its Arabian Baths, we know nothing of how it came to acquire its landmark status or what place it holds in the wider culture and civic life of Zubrowka. We do not even know much about its layout and its architecture: though the bright pink and highly ornamented façade gives the hotel the very look of a dollhouse, the building is never actually given the kind of schematic dollhouse treatment that Anderson uses to great effect in navigating through the *Belafonte* in *The Life Aquatic* or the Bishop home in *Moonrise Kingdom*. Only very briefly do we even go inside any of the guest rooms of the hotel. Nor do we know much of the people who work there. Among the film's many hotel staff members, only Gustave's (Ralph Fiennes) immediate lieutenant Mr. Mosher (Larry Pine) is ever named; aside from the lesser concierges who mark the hotel's steady decline as they each take over the institution's main position in succession, the remainder of the employees are left anonymous and consigned largely to the background of the story.

Insofar as Anderson's film gives the impression of affording us a rich window into the candy-colored world of the Grand Budapest, that view is effected almost entirely through the figure of M. Gustave, the esteemed concierge and reigning impresario of the beloved operation. Gustave is the hotel and the hotel is Gustave, a transposition of identities between person and place that is made quite literal at various points in the film. "I apologize on behalf of the hotel," Gustave declares after insulting Zero in a brief fit of rage, worried that his conduct "is beneath the standards of the Grand Budapest"—this after he has just escaped from prison and is no longer employed by or affiliated with the institution in any formal way at all. For Gustave himself as for so many others in the world of the film, his person and that place—at least, that is, the *idea* of that place—are effectively inseparable. "I began to realize that many of the hotel's most valued and distinguished guests—came for *him*," Zero reflects in his old age. This is not the first such identification in Anderson's filmmaking, and to a certain extent Gustave is but the latest entry in a long line of presiding father figures in the filmmaker's body of work. Royal Tenenbaum, though he lives in exile from his own home and family, nevertheless gives his name to both the Tenenbaum house and to the family members who live there, over whom he still feels ownership. Steve Zissou likewise imposes his own name and his own set of rules (and dress code) on the members of Team Zissou and the floating world apart that they create on the *Belafonte*. Mr. Henry imposed his own quirky order on the members of his gang and the rambling warehouse where they lived. And even Max Fischer tries to make himself synonymous with Rushmore, either adopting or inventing an elaborate emblazoned uniform all his own.

But although Gustave shares certain characteristics with these forebears, he is ultimately a leader of a very different sort within Anderson's filmography. Like many of those figures before him, he demands direct control over deciding who can and cannot be allowed into the Grand Budapest family: He is the arbiter of membership, the collector figure to this most esteemed collection of service professionals. "Am I to understand you've surreptitiously hired this young man in the position of a Lobby Boy?" he asks Mr. Mosher in horror after discovering Zero in full uniform without ever having been consulted. He promptly proceeds to interview him all over again on the spot. And like other previous Anderson impresarios (Zissou especially), Gustave imposes strict rules of conduct and a meticulous dress code on his subordinates, chiding them for even the smallest lapses in etiquette or blemishes on their careful coiffure. "Should I discover a lapse of any variety," he says to his subordinates, "I promise: swift and merciless justice will descend upon you." Yet if Gustave shares these characteristics with his Andersonian forbearers, he differs in one very important way: he doesn't actually believe in any of it, not for a moment. The great charm of M. Gustave for those who know him intimately is that he understands his place at the pinnacle of the Grand Budapest to be fundamentally an act of performance, a role that he entirely relishes but never actually believes to be real. Outside the earshot of the hotel's precious guests, he curses with abandon, throwing around the most vulgar language with such style that it borders on artistry. He offers his esteemed guests earnest promises of personal service, vowing, "I'll see to it myself immediately" before shunting the assigned task to the hotel's lowliest staff as soon as the guests have moved on. A flawless guardian of taste in his professional life, he has no trouble offering extremely candid appraisals of the culture and people around him when he is alone with a confidant, calling most of the highly prized art collection of the Family Desgoffe-und-Taxis "worthless junk" when no one else is around. Gustave is a figure who both cherishes the culture and civilization entrusted in some small part to his safekeeping and actually values them not at all. He is the collector figure described by Benjamin who possesses exquisite taste and at the same time is always haunted by the vulgarian who says "All these paintings are very pretty—but they're dormant capital" (*Arcades* 209). Hence Gustave's mercurial reaction to the famous painting "Boy with Apple," bequeathed to him by his hotel guest and lover Madame Céline Villeneuve Desgoffe-und-Taxis, known as Madame D (Tilda Swinton). "I'll never part with it," he says at first. "It reminded her of me. It will remind me of her. Always. I'll die with this picture above my bed." But only moments later, he changes course entirely. "Actually, we should sell it. Sooner rather than later. . . . We'll contact the black market and liquidate 'Boy with Apple' by the end of the week then leave the country and lay low somewhere along the Maltese Riviera." Gustave's relationship to the Grand Budapest itself is much the same. He professes to esteem it above all else in the world and proclaims it to his staff to be "a great and noble house placed under your protection," and he also is ready to leave it recklessly at a moment's notice if he thinks he can find a plausible way to live out an existence of free-flowing "whores and whiskey," a life as thoroughly debauched as his current life is impeccably cultivated.

Gustave's fundamental detachment from the world around him and even from his own esteemed place in it ultimately gives him tremendous power. Holding nothing sacred, he also is beholden to nothing and to no one. He effectively steals from the Desgoffe-und-Taxises knowing full well the family's penchant for violence, and he successfully challenges or manipulates the nation's military officers, police officers, and court officials at various points in the film. Locked away in a Zubrowkan prison on trumped-up charges of murdering Madame D., Gustave very quickly becomes as valued within the criminal social world of the prison as he was within the high-class ecosystem of the hotel. "When you find yourself in a place like this, you must never be a candy-ass. You've got to prove yourself from Day One," he tells Zero, but his real secret is something less than physically brutal. Gustave is charmingly polite to the other prisoners and begins treating them much like the guests at his old hotel not because he has suddenly become a concierge of the people but because, fundamentally, he never rated the hotel guests as being much better than these riff-raff in the first place. His act is not really any different, it's just being performed in a different theater. Likewise Gustave's endearing willingness to give credit where credit is due—praising the prison slop as "quite warm and nourishing this morning" or noting the artistic talent evident in an inmate's escape drawings. "*Very* good. You've got a wonderful line, Ludwig." It's not that Ludwig (Harvey Keitel) is to Gustave as talented as, say, Johannes van Hoytl the Younger, the fictitious master painter behind "Boy with Apple" and the only other artist to whom he offers praise in the film; rather, van Hoytl is to Gustave probably in the end not that much better than Ludwig. Gustave knows what taste dictates that he should say and in the right company he is perfectly willing to say it. He will even occasionally wax eloquent about a cultural object that he honestly believes has some intrinsic value, noting the beauty of "van Hoytl's exquisite portrayal of a beautiful boy on the cusp of manhood." But that won't stop him from trying to sell the thing if he thinks he can profit from it. In the end, five-star hotel soup and prison mush are pretty much the same to him; the only real question is what praising or disparaging them can do for him in that moment. It must be remembered that, paeans to the greatness of the Grand Budapest aside, Gustave makes his living in the hotel trade. He is not steward to some grand imperial palace or chief of staff in some great government ministry; he is a showman at a spa town offering a little bit of luxury and refinement at a steep price, premised on the governing logic that everyone will keep on moving and their stay will only be temporary. To be sure, Gustave offers more of himself in this role than most are willing to, in just about every way. "I go to bed with all my friends," he says in reference to his well-known penchant for sleeping with even the most aged of the wealthy dowagers who visit his hotel. But that doesn't mean he won't see them out the door when their time is up. "Time to go!" he jauntily exclaims to Madame D. when the scheduled time of her departure has arrived, this even after she has confided in him her fear that if she leaves, "this may be the last time we ever see each other."

At bottom, Gustave is an exceedingly lonely man. His world is one of endless transience, a grand palace full of people who are always leaving. He has his staff, to be sure, but his relationship with them is decidedly held at arm's length, a fact that can be measured by the sudden closeness and intensity of his very different working relationship with Zero. This master of the great institution of the Grand Budapest—effectively the organization's head and leader, as the actual owner of the hotel is unknown—lives by himself in a tiny windowless garret on the upper floors of the building, where he takes his meals alone. Anderson in fact pictures him doing so once, offset to the far right of the frame closed in by blank and imposing walls, drinking soup at a little table in his undergarments, as though he had no other clothes besides his hotel uniform. Gustave may regard that spotless garment as a kind of costume and may derive great power from that level of actorly detachment, but that does not mean he actually has any other roles to play in his life. It is in this context that we can begin to understand the intensity of the relationship that Gustave very quickly develops with Zero and the matched pair that the two almost immediately form. Almost from the moment of their first interview, Gustave detects something different and uniquely appealing about this new lobby boy—only minutes after they have first met he entrusts him with two equally sacred tasks, the lighting of a candle in the Cathedral of Santa Maria Christiana and the procurement of pastries from the beloved Mendl's. As we learn later in Anderson's montage introduction to the Society of the Crossed Keys, a kind of fraternal order of luxury hotel concierges, it is incumbent upon Gustave as a great concierge to identify a protégé to support him in his work, one who is capable of taking on all manner of high-stakes responsibilities at a moment's notice—whether tasting the day's soup, performing cardiopulmonary resuscitation, or directing a fire brigade. Why Gustave has waited so long into his career to find a protégé we cannot know, though we may presume that he had simply not yet found the right candidate. (We are given no indication in the film that he is a serial mentor in the same way that he is a serial lover.) What we do know is that Zero offers Gustave something unique that deeply resonates with his own lonely circumstance: a complete and utter lack of outside attachments beyond the world of the hotel. With no family and no friends to speak of at the film's outset, no professional ties nor even any nation to call his own, Zero presents to Gustave a picture of potential devotion to the idea of the Grand Budapest as complete and unadulterated as his own—which is to say, for Gustave, a picture of potential devotion to himself. Asking Zero at the end of his impromptu interview "Why do you want to be a Lobby Boy?" Gustave is charmed by his response, so simple it is almost evasive. "Well, who *wouldn't*—at the Grand Budapest, sir?" Lots of people, surely. The implication immediately understood by interviewer and interviewee alike is that those people don't really count.

Essentially, Zero professes—and very quickly delivers—an absolute promise of commitment, which raises the question of exactly what kind of relationship Gustave and Zero truly have. Surely the easiest summary would be one of mentor and protégé, except that the intensity of their coupling extends far beyond the boundaries of the hotel itself and even well beyond the extremities of the hotelier profession. Even as Gustave suffers incarceration and becomes a fugitive, Zero stays by his side. Even when Gustave declares of the Grand Budapest with no small amount of melodrama, "I shall never cross its threshold again in my lifetime," Zero never questions that his place is with his former boss. It is the rare mentor-and-protégé pair indeed who think it appropriate to plot together to escape from their jobs and live a ribald life on the Maltese Riviera instead. The utter transportability of Gustave and Zero's partnership—one that literally takes them from the depths of the Zubrowka prison system to the heights of the Zubrowkan Alps—speaks to a level of closeness that goes beyond the professional. It surely isn't fatherly, at least not in any traditional sense of the word—that promise of shared "whores and whiskey" points to something else at once more intimate and more equal. At one point, Zero's fiancée Agatha (Saoirse Ronan) speaks of the two as brothers—"two radiant, celestial brothers," to be exact, in the purple language of the romantic poem she is reciting—and this seems to come closer to the truth despite the great age difference between the two.

But as with the so-called brotherhood between Zissou and Esteban, the fraternal marker seems to mask something fundamentally erotic in the relationship. It is not that the partnership of Gustave and Zero is ever explicitly sexual—though Gustave is rumored to be bisexual and though he boasts "I go to bed with all my friends," Zero does not seem to be included in that tally. But Gustave exercises over Zero an unusual degree of control on matters of intimacy, a level of interference against which Zero initially objects but to which he eventually acquiesces. Gustave deems it his right to inquisition Agatha when he learns of her budding relationship with Zero, explaining to his sulking friend "I'm only interviewing this vision of loveliness on *your* behalf." Only with Gustave's permission can their amorous relationship proceed, a level of authority literalized later in the film when Gustave is seen officiating at their wedding. Gustave clearly sees Zero's intimate life to be very much his business, and for all of his verbal protests against this interference Zero surely understands on some level where Gustave is coming from, as he himself values Gustave more than his own lover. Though Zero's only formal relationship to Gustave is that of supervisor and employee, when his friend is falsely sent to prison Zero not only risks his own life in helping Gustave escape but enlists his fiancée and asks her to likewise risk her own life. Zero stands side by side with Gustave solving the mystery of Madame D.'s murder and battling her sociopathic son's sociopathic hired thug, never once contemplating that his greatest loyalties might more properly belong elsewhere. Rather, he praises Agatha profusely for her fearlessness, recalling with relish that "she was also very brave" and explaining that "she was born that way," when all the while the sole measure of that bravery is the series of risks Zero explicitly asks her to undertake for the benefit of his friend Gustave—sneaking past soldiers, running from active gunfire, hanging off the side of the Grand Budapest façade. It is one thing to risk your own life for a dear friend, quite another to demand that your fiancée do the same.

The fact that Agatha is willing to even take on these death-defying missions speaks to the nature of the bond that she recognizes between the man that she loves and the man that he loves in turn. Despite their manifold differences in age, race, nationality, professional standing, and even physical stature, there is a fundamental likeness between Gustave and Zero, a kernel of similarity that binds them together in a way in which they are bound to no others. Like so many Anderson characters before them, Gustave and Zero are both remarkably isolated in the world at the film's beginning, effectively or literally familyless and bereft of any real and lasting friends. They have at their fingertips the makings of a collective identity and a constructed family unit of a kind that would have enticed so many other Anderson figures: one can only imagine what Max Fischer might make of the Grand Budapest and the apparent opportunities it provides for meaning and belonging. Yet neither of them actually takes the institution seriously in that way at all, utterly rejecting as an impossible fantasy the idea that meaning can be found in such instances of collectivity—it's a performance only, as Gustave well knows. Instead, these two men find meaning and belonging in each other, recognizing the potential power of the perfectly matched pair even in the face of a much larger but less meaningful possible collection. Together, they both finally find a place where they each belong: not an absolute place of the kind represented by the physical structure of the Grand Budapest itself, but a relative place, next to one another. Side by side, they each finally have a spot in the world where they perfectly fit: on a windswept toboggan together, atop a pastoral haystack, or lying side by side in adjacent beds in a railcar, framed in a perfectly symmetrical top shot in a manner that Anderson usually reserves for lovers and married couples (fig. 23).

What Gustave gives to Zero besides himself in this arrangement is the more obvious exchange: the idea of the Grand Budapest and all that it represents, all the history and tradition of a national landmark for a young man who has lost his own home and nation. What Zero gives to

Figure 23. A matched pair

Gustave is somewhat more mysterious but arguably more powerful. A friendless and familyless man who makes his living in a hotel, Gustave is a figure surrounded by and perhaps obsessed by transience. We might even say that he is a figure who is somewhat in love with death itself—how else to explain the great pleasure he openly derives from sleeping with elderly women in the very last years of their lives or the final kiss he gives to Madame D.'s corpse at her wake. Gustave's great dream of escape is a fantasy of prostitutes and alcohol, a life defined by attachmentless sex and perpetual inebriation: it is ultimately a dream of self-annihilation. In Zero, he finds something to believe in and something to live for—the strength of this commitment being measured by his willingness to die for his friend in the end. Hence the scene of Gustave's tragic and untimely demise in an impromptu execution by the military during a rail stop. Gustave's death is presented by the older Zero as a fatal instance of overreach by a man who is used to charming everyone he meets, the moment when, in the elder Zero's words, the "faint glimmers of civilization" still remaining at that time finally came face to face with "this barbaric slaughterhouse that was once known as humanity." In Zero's own reading of the incident, Gustave's demise is a measure of just how much the cultivated world his friend and mentor once knew has been swept away by history, and to this end the scene is almost an exact replay of an earlier confrontation where Gustave and Zero were likewise accosted by soldiers on a rail stop but in which Gustave's appeal on Zero's behalf was warmly received by a genteel intervening commander. But to view Gustave's death in this way is arguably to be fooled a bit too much by the great concierge's great performance of civility. Gustave often has relied on his charms in a scrape, to be sure. But he also is far too cunning and far too fundamentally uncivilized than to use charm as his only tool. He has faced no shortage of brutes before, from the various inmates in prison to Dmitri Desgoffe-und-Taxis (Adrien Brody) and his henchman, and he always has had an impeccable sense of when to charm and when to fight and when to simply run away. Gustave's confrontation with the brutish soldier in the railcar is not so much a rare instance of misjudgment as it is a deliberate decision to try to save Zero's life, knowing one of the two of them must die to appease these uniformed monsters. Gustave has been in bed with death for a long time, and he arguably knew exactly what he was doing in courting the ire of that soldier. Whether Zero truly gains anything from this sacrifice is another question, for the figure of him in the film's second framing story, as an old man wandering the hotel like a ghost, is among the saddest in Anderson's body of work. Zero has survived the turmoil of the war and after that the era of Soviet occupation that followed—an age in which the forced collectivism of the Communists has perverted and destroyed the very concepts of collectivity on which so much of Anderson's aesthetic is founded, turning the glorious eccentricity of the prewar Grand Budapest into the brutalist relic the older Zero (F. Murray Abraham) now mournfully inhabits. Like so many other Anderson characters before him, Zero is stuck in an earlier time, his traumas from that bygone era have petrified and never closed—Gustave's death as well as that of Agatha and his newborn son, both of whom died of "an absurd little disease" called "the Prussian grippe." Zero claims he has maintained ownership of the hotel, which he inherited from Gustave, as a testament not to his mentor and soulmate but to his young wife. "The hotel I keep for Agatha," he says. "We were happy here. For a little while." But then again, Zero always has displaced the erotics of his attachment to Gustave onto his relationship with Agatha, leaving one to wonder for which of his loves he truly is still in mourning. What is certain is that he has turned the Grand Budapest into a tomb. It is perhaps an inevitable fulfillment of Gustave's own infatuation with transience and with death, a literalization of the role that the hotel always partly played for him. But it also is a violation of the spirit of Anderson's filmmaking and the ethos of collecting it extols. Zero has reduced his once sizable portfolio of properties to a single holding. In the narrator's words, "Zero Moustafa had traded a great and important fortune in exchange for one costly, unprofitable, doomed hotel." He has turned away from the logic of the collection, which is about rebuilding and remaking, to that of the souvenir, an unchanging token of the past, an object that promises not a mastery over or departure from history but an endless and frozen obsession with it. Like so many Anderson characters before him, he is immobilized by trauma, but on a much grander scale. He is only one half of a matched pair, and he will never be complete.

Collecting Wes Anderson

Anderson's Collected Works

In remarking on his own body of films, Anderson once observed that "There are a lot of things that, from one movie to the next, are related. . . . I like the idea of, after I make some more movies, they can all sit on a shelf together and they sort of fit together" (Horowitz). It is a comment essentially on the dynamics of the collection that his films in total form, an oblique acknowledgment of the Benjaminian "magic circle" that makes the films together take on meanings and significances that they do not each hold alone. The dynamics in part result from the continuity of Anderson's visual universe and the compatibility of his characterological interests across films: the same continuity that has prompted a notable subgenre of Anderson-inspired visual art that focuses on mixing and matching scenes and characters from different Anderson films together in a single composition. Max Dalton's cover artwork for *The Wes Anderson Collection* is one such example, placing together at one city intersection the Hinckley Cold Storage station from *Bottle Rocket*, the Rushmore Academy, the Tenenbaum townhouse, and *Moonrise Kingdom*'s Fort Lebanon. The banner artwork on the Rushmore Academy website, a central Internet repository for all things Anderson, is another, bringing together Mr. Fox, Steve Zissou, Sam Shakusky and Suzy Bishop, Max Fischer, and Richie Tenenbaum in one combined tableau defined by the Grand Budapest Hotel on one side and the motel from *Bottle Rocket* on the other. Placed alongside one another on the DVD shelf of the cinephile (or the personal Netflix or Amazon Prime library these days, as the case may be), Anderson's films begin to speak to each other and inspire connections that enrich them all. What might Max Fischer, that master of the extracurricular, make of the Khaki Scouts were he to summer on New Penzance Island? How would Jack Whitman comport himself in an extended stay at the Grand Budapest Hotel rather than the Hotel Chevalier? What if Royal Tenenbaum and the Bishops from *Moonrise Kingdom* found themselves litigating against one another in court?

Today we might call these questions of universing, a kind of hipster alternative to the recombinatory powers of the various Marvel superheroes and their variously overlapping Marvel superworlds. They are questions, that is, of fandom. For Henry Jenkins, media fan culture represents at heart "the application of folk culture practices to mass cultural content," a form of nonconsumerist production achieved "through the appropriation and transformation of materials borrowed from mass culture" (246). From very early in his career, Anderson has encouraged such appropriation and transformation, modeling it in the films themselves and the ways in which they slyly revisit and revise one another's characters and themes. If, in other words, the aftermarket ephemera of paintings and websites prompt us to ask expanded-universe questions of Anderson's filmic worlds, it is in part because Anderson's films themselves prompt their own series of metafilmic questions via their self-conscious design as a collected (and collectible) body of work. "I do feel a bit like my characters from one movie could walk into another one of my movies and it would make sense," Anderson has said in interviews (Desplechin), happily admitting the possibilities of an active fandom culture that will fancifully remix his different worlds in hodge-podge arrangements from online fan films to Etsy art displays.[18]

The fact that such recombinations are already hard-wired into Anderson's films is part of the point and part of the fun, with the director himself laying the groundwork for fan expansion by way of the distinctive and highly self-referential casting choices that run from picture to picture and that all but demand we pay attention to the possible links between the works. Anderson's films are often described as having an ensemble or repertory quality, so frequent are some of his collaborations with key actors. Bill Murray, for instance, has appeared in some capacity in every Anderson film since *Rushmore*; Owen Wilson has acted in six out of eight (to say nothing of the fact that he collaborated on the writing of three of them); Jason Schwartzman has featured in five and in several of Anderson's commercials and shorts. The logic of Anderson's casting decisions explicitly asks us to draw connections across the diegetic borders of the pictures and to carry through thematic concerns and even narrative lines from one film to another. In *The Life Aquatic*, for instance, Bill Murray as the aquarium-building Herman Blume from *Rushmore* is reborn as the ocean-voyaging Steve Zissou, both figures set adrift by the surprising demands of a younger male claiming to be their son in some way. Owen Wilson as Dignan from *Bottle Rocket* appears again and again as a figure desperate to be let into some greater family unit he idealizes—as Eli Cash wishing he could be a Tenenbaum in *The Royal Tenenbaums*, as Ned Plimpton joining Team Zissou in *The Life Aquatic*, as Francis Whitman trying to reunite and rekindle his own family in *The Darjeeling Limited*. Anjelica Huston plays both sides of a Janus-faced mother: the endlessly accommodating Etheline Tenenbaum, ready to readmit her children back into the family home at the least provocation, and the pathologically distant Patricia Whitman, committed to permanently escaping from her children and ensuring they have no home anywhere in the world. And Ed Norton patrols the borderlands of Anderson's filmic universes as the goodhearted but ineffectual Scoutmaster Ward in *Moonrise Kingdom* and the equally goodhearted and equally ineffectual Inspector Henckels in *The Grand Budapest Hotel*, offering a rare example of humanity and humility trying to exist inside overwhelmingly militaristic organizations. And then there are the actors who appear like hidden Easter eggs in the background roles of Anderson's films: the Indian juggler and plate-spinner Kumar Pallana, who appears in minor roles or cameos in almost every Anderson film from *Bottle Rocket* through *The Darjeeling Limited*; or Pallana's son Dipak, who has cameo appearances in Anderson's first three films; or the actor Waris Ahluwalia, who first appeared in *The Life Aquatic* and Anderson's subsequent American Express commercial and then took on the diegetically jarring task of playing different roles in *The Darjeeling Limited* and its precursor short *Hotel Chevalier* before joining the Society of the Crossed Keys in *Grand Budapest*. *The Grand Budapest Hotel* even makes a kind of joke of these perpetual reappearances, with many of the Khaki Scouts from *Moonrise Kingdom* taking on minor parts as lobby boys and service attendants in that film and almost the entirety of the Society of the Crossed Keys membership hailing from earlier Anderson works.

These actorly interchanges between Anderson's films make literal what Benjamin always saw as one of the primary facets of the collection's power: its ability to make independent objects "come together . . . to form a whole magic encyclopedia, a world order" (*Arcades* 207). Although each film is able to stand alone and independent from the others, they grow richer and more elaborate when placed in one another's company. The films ask their viewers to regard them as a group, encouraging us to read across the diegetic boundaries of each filmic world. Anderson cultivates an aesthetics of collection within his films and an ethos of collection among his films: He all but asks for his works to be collected. This dynamic is nowhere more apparent than in the extensive extrafilmic materials that Anderson personally curates to accompany each of his films in their posttheatrical afterlives. As Orgeron notes, Anderson came of age as a director at the dawn of the DVD age and the ethos of the DVD feature is built into his approach to marketing and distributing his works. "The development of Anderson's cinematic authorship, in fact, coincides with the birth and refinement of DVD technology," Orgeron writes, and the filmmaker's personal involvement in the creation of those DVDs yields a "complex rhetorical structure" that "projects a carefully authored public image of himself as author" (43). All Anderson's films through *Moonrise Kingdom* are available today on DVD through the Criterion Collection (a *Grand Budapest* edition is rumored to be in the works), Criterion being the company that first pioneered the DVD feature as an enticement to cinephile film collectors.[19] Even within the feature-rich environment of the Criterion catalog, Anderson's works stand out for their superabundance of ancillary material. To take only one example, the Criterion edition of *The Darjeeling Limited* devotes an entire second disc to special features and promises the following:

> Behind-the-scenes documentary by Barry Braverman; Discussion between Anderson and filmmaker James Ivory on the music used in the film; Anderson's American Express commercial; On-set footage shot by Coppola and actor Waris Ahluwalia; Video essay by film writer Matt Zoller Seitz; Audition footage; Deleted and alternate scenes; Stills galleries from James Hamilton, Laura Wilson, and Sylvia Plachy; An insert featuring an essay by critic Richard Brody and original illustrations by Eric Chase Anderson.

Other entries in the Anderson DVD library go even further afield in their offerings. The *Royal Tenenbaums* DVD, for instance, includes a "collectible insert" featuring room-by-room drawings of the Tenenbaum house as well as an example of just how far afield a DVD extra may fall from the narrative core of the film in Anderson's conception of apropos features: It includes an NPR radio segment on the Mexican artist Miguel Calderón, who was not involved in the making of the film at all but whose artwork was featured on the walls of Eli Cash's apartment in Anderson's *mise-en-scène*.

In essence, Anderson positions himself through these carefully cultivated materials as a kind of collector's collector: both a figure who knows how to inspire the film collector's acquisitive impulse (leveraging in full force what Benjamin provocatively calls "the sex appeal of the inorganic" [*Arcades* 79]) and a collector himself who uses the venue of the DVD feature to welcome his fans into the world of some of his own collections, Calderón's paintings included. With the displacement of the DVD by the Internet, Anderson has adapted much of this operation to the online presences of his films. *Moonrise Kingdom* and *The Grand Budapest Hotel* both yielded elaborate websites that have remained active long after the films have left the theaters, offering such features as a guided tour of New Penzance Island or educational videos on the history of Anderson's invented European nation offered via a fictional outfit called the Akademie Zubrowka. Insofar as these features have become an essential part of Anderson's filmic identity in what Orgeron calls the "cinematic aftermarket" (43), they also, he argues, have become one of the primary means by which Anderson struggles with his own problematic status as a film auteur. For Orgeron, the concomitant rise of the DVD with Anderson's career beginnings created a unique moment of paradox in the history of auteurist reception. On the one hand, Orgeron argues, "DVD technology is, in fact, largely responsible for the inauguration of a new age of the cinematic author, returning like all repressed things do, with new vigor and omnipotence" (58), a return abetted by the sudden ubiquity of features like the director's commentary and the director's cut and what Orgeron calls "tome-like and lionizing essays" (58) focused on the director. At the same time, Orgeron explains, the era of the DVD has undercut the romantic image of "the lone figure making his . . . films despite the system" that marked "the auteur of Sarris's era"; in this new era of the auteur, the film consumer is overrun "with images of overpopulated sets filled with cast and crew, interviews with and commentary by cinematographers, costumers, set designers, and the like" (59).

If we can think of Anderson as a kind of DVD native as a filmmaker, then we also can regard this general paradox that many directors faced as playing a particularly acute role in Anderson's own self-conception and self-creation as a filmmaker with a notable public profile. (Indeed, Anderson's quixotic journey to Massachusetts to personally screen *Rushmore* for Pauline Kael bespeaks nothing if not a troubled relationship with auteurism and with his own perceived identity as an auteur. There is perhaps no greater paradox in action than to make such a point of personally screening your film for Kael, who was always a vehement critic of auteurist theory.) In Orgeron's view, Anderson has long used the DVD feature as a way to escape the totalizing myth of the pure auteur, offering his many collaborators abundant space to explain and present their work. "Anderson," he writes, "has participated in a method of self-representation that makes his *dependence* on others a proud thing. . . . In the age of the new Auteur, Anderson has used its primary weapon to reflect back less upon the mythic and mythically elusive author himself . . . and has opted, rather, to reflect upon the author's tenuous fit within a larger community" (59). Anderson is no doubt a figure who particularly cherishes the collaborative aspects of the filmmaking process—so much so, in fact, that he has a pet peeve about members of his cast or crew ever actually leaving the set of his films. Not unlike his own character of Steve Zissou, Anderson wants the team to stay together at all times. "I like working with a group," he says. "I don't like people going away to trailers and things like that. I like everybody to just stay together" (Seitz 265). Yet within the aesthetic framework of the collection, it is perhaps inevitable that such collaboration—no matter how sincerely it is enacted or how explicit its role in crafting his films is made—will reflect back on Anderson individually. The collection, as Stewart reminds us, is always ultimately a personal expression of the collector, "the narrative of the collection" being in the end synonymous with "the narrative of the individual subject—that is, the collector himself" (156). As curator of his DVD features and as the guiding force in selecting and securing his own collaborators, Anderson's attempts to diffuse authorship throughout multiple aspects of the filmmaking process ultimately throw refracted light back on his originary position in that system.

Building the Collection: Anderson's Method of Production

In other words, the collector always stands at the center of the collection, at least figuratively if not literally. And in fact the actual conditions of Anderson's production arrangements make clear the degree to which he exercises his collector's prerogative in calling together and determining the arrangement of the multifarious aspects of his filmic worlds—that is, the degree to which he actively assumes the central auteurist position that becomes somewhat obfuscated amid the clutter and cacophony of his manifold DVD features. "He is such an auteur director," remarked one collaborator on *The Grand Budapest Hotel*. "He pays attention to every little thing. . . . It's the same with every department. He's quite particular"—and this coming from the film's graphic designer, Ashleigh Kane, whose job it was to execute the various print typefaces diegetically used within the picture. Anderson clearly values and exults in collaboration, from the beginning stages of his filmmaking process to the last. Every single one of his screenplays, from *Bottle Rocket* to *Budapest*, has been written collaboratively, for instance. But even here Anderson insists that he is the one "who does the physical writing" in those relationships. "I'm putting it into words. The rest of the collaboration is endless talking" (Blume). Although important, such collaborations are, to Anderson, ultimately only instigations to his own, singular artistic energies.

Those energies are fundamentally those of a collector, a figure who finds the route to artistic expression through the selection and arrangement of the preexisting more than through the whole-cloth creation of the new. Upon first finishing a screenplay, Anderson's earliest production collaborations are typically with Randy Poster, his long-time music supervisor, and Adam Stockhausen, his current production designer and former art director. Together, this coterie works to build through complementary processes the sonic and the visual landscapes of the film to come. "We're doing different research all at once," as Anderson put it to one interviewer (Karpel). In fact, the nature of these processes is quite literally one of collection—of accretion, culling, and arrangement, of curating the choicest works from a superabundance of visual and sonic possibilities. Anderson's goal in preproduction, as he has explained in interviews, is to accrue "millions of images" so that he and Stockhausen can "start looking at them together, and I say, 'I like this. I like this. I like this'" (Roberts). Then, when the process of what Anderson calls "gathering and shaping" those images has gone through multiple iterations, Anderson and Stockhausen take the final set of images and, as Stockhausen has explained, "lay that all out on a gigantic table and start breaking apart what's a set, what's a location, what's a miniature build, what's a painting, what's whatever, and work through step by step by step" (Roberts). What is remarkable about this process is the degree to which it relies not on invention but on selection. According to Anderson, nearly every last detail of his filmic worlds is drawn from an external referent that is either used directly or painstakingly recreated with greater or lesser degrees of fidelity. Even the background hallways of the Grand Budapest Hotel are essentially borrowed in this manner: "We had Ingmar Bergman's *The Silence* because it's set in a hotel in a made up Eastern European country and [had] a train and all that sort of stuff," he recalled. "In fact, we made their hotel corridors. His are in black and white so we had to guess" (Roberts). Anderson's preproduction strategy should be immediately recognizable as one of collection building, of accumulating, selecting, and arranging the visual world of his films.

Having built the visual structure of his world in his design-first process and overlaid a sense of mood in his collaborations with Poster, Anderson next turns his attention to planning in meticulous detail the cinematographic presentation of that world. Frame by painstaking frame, Anderson sketches out the movement of his film in an elaborate system of storyboards inclusive of the already determined properties and costumes as well as the fundamentals of camera position and editing cuts. "It's a way to figure out what goes where and how it all fits together and how we're going to construct it as well as how we're going to shoot it," Anderson explains (Karpel). Most directors storyboard to some degree; some even do so to quite an elaborate extent, though typically with far bigger budgets and far greater spectacle than the typical Anderson film. But few can match the meticulous precision of Anderson's cartoon version of his films-to-be. Since the creation of *Fantastic Mr. Fox*, Anderson has even become accustomed to crafting fully operational animatics, or rough animations, from his storyboards, voicing all the parts himself. "I have somebody else redraw [the storyboards] better," he explains, "and they do lots of panels and poses so that we can then animate them, and then we record a soundtrack which consists of me doing voices. Sometimes, music goes there as well. We make the movie as a cartoon" (Stern). Very little is left to chance on an Anderson film shoot; seeing the animatic for *Budapest* before shooting, Willem Dafoe recalls thinking "This guy doesn't even need actors. The film is already made" (Fox). If, as Stewart argues, the arrangement and exhibition of the items of the collection is the point at which the collection truly comes into being—or, as she says, "To ask which principles of organization are used in articulating the collection is to begin to discern what the collection is about" (154)—then it is little wonder that Anderson should aim to exert as much control over this feature of his filmmaking as possible, for it is in the process of exhibiting his collection that it will finally come alive. "I've done a bunch of movies," Anderson has said. "And it's a luxury to me that they're all whatever I've wanted them to be" (Lamont).

For Anderson himself, there seems to be no question but that he is the ultimate author of his films. He is simply an author of a very particular type: one who prefers to work in and through the processes of collection—and thus, correspondingly, the collective. More than one Anderson collaborator has remarked on the strikingly communal feeling of the Anderson set. "It becomes like summer camp or like school—you bond," recalled one crew member. "And that, by osmosis, makes the films better" (Lamont). In contrast to the typical arrangements of the highly diffuse and painstakingly microscheduled production shoots of most major films, Anderson asks his cast and crew to work and live on equal footing during their time together, booking his cast members, his production designer, his director of photography, and his costume designer into the same hotel and filling that space with ephemera evocative of the film itself. On *The Grand Budapest Hotel* he even went so far as to commission oil portraits of the major cast members in costume simply to hang around the corridors of their living space. "A mood thing," as one observer called it (Lamont). And always, Anderson reports, there are the traces of the original collection from which the film itself began, a vast communal repository of images, films, books, and other material that helped inspire the design of the film and that Anderson makes available to his collaborators throughout the shoot. "It's just that everybody is there together and I've got all this stuff that I've been looking at," he explains. "It's just, 'Here's the stuff that relates to the movie that we've got if you're interested.' And literally, it's sitting on a table there and people come by and take a movie [to watch]" (Roberts). Such efforts purposefully blur the line between the shooting day and the rest of the time spent on location, enveloping cast and crew alike in an approximation of the totalizing worlds of the films themselves. Which is to say, they envelop the cast and crew in Anderson's own imaginative space, making them one more part of the total collection he is building. Insofar as Anderson's films always deal with the problems and possibilities of the collector's impulse and the issues of the human collective, family or otherwise, so too does Anderson enact these same concerns within the production processes of his filmmaking. As one of the director's former production designers once observed, Anderson's shoots bear a remarkable resemblance to Anderson's fictions: "It's always a thing about a guy who's kind of nuts and in charge, and a gang of people who do his bidding and get into trouble" (Dean).

Anderson is not unaware of the inherent humor in this arrangement, of the micromanaging maestro dependent upon and indebted to the work of the collective, and in fact this tension becomes the central comic conceit of his much-beloved American Express commercial. The piece is endearingly self-deprecating, making it seem a wonder that Anderson's films ever get made at all. His film production process as depicted in that short is almost unmanageably chaotic: in the span of two minutes no fewer than nine collaborators approach Anderson with suggestions, questions, and requests related to everything from line readings to script changes to prop design to cinematographic choices. Anderson's navigation of this onslaught is equal parts confident and inept: his own contributions to the film range from the hopelessly opaque ("It sounds fake," he repeatedly tells a bewildered actor) to the comically absurd ("Can you do a 357 [handgun] with a bayonet?"). To the extent that Anderson's films have any value, the short seems to suggest, that value happens around or in spite of Anderson's own presence on the set. Yet the mark of the auteur, whether desired or not, is inescapable. The commercial is part of the "My Life, My Card" series, placing the director's claim of ownership front and center. And the Anderson character that Anderson plays in the short is almost obsessively possessive about every element of his filmic world, his dialogue constantly punctuated by references to his ownership over the shoot: "I'll do it. I got it"; "I'm going to sit there. What are you doing there?"; "Were those my birds? I need those." Whatever the realities of on-set collaboration may be, Anderson stands inescapably at the center of those efforts. The collector is always found in every item of his collection, each element selected and arranged in such a way as to reveal some aspect of his very consciousness and being. Or, as Stewart said of the collection, "Each sign is placed in relation to a chain of signifiers whose ultimate referent is not the interior of the room . . . but the interior of the self" (158). It is an ethos that Seitz all but makes explicit in explaining the title of his sizable tome of Anderson interviews, *The Wes Anderson Collection*. "It's called *The Wes Anderson Collection* because the result reminded me of Margot's library in *The Royal Tenenbaums*, Steve Zissou's floating laboratory/film studio in *The Life Aquatic*, or Suzy Bishop's collection of stolen library books in *Moonrise Kingdom*. It's a tour of an artist's mind, with the artist as guide and amiable companion" (26). Chaotic or orderly, communal or command-driven, Anderson's filmmaking is always a process of building and displaying a collection, of building and displaying a self.

The Collector as Author

And like all collections, what it demands in return for this display is the promise of some viewer, some potential audience to its wonders. Indeed the very act of starting a collection "depends upon the creation of an individual perceiving and apprehending the collection," as Stewart (154) reminds us. The collection is always an act of communication, whether directly in the moment at which the collector opens the curio cabinet or over great expanses of time as the collection is transmitted across generations. This promise of revelation for a return promise of transmission stands at the center of Anderson's works. It is an exchange that is implicit in almost any film but one that is made visually explicit and thematically central in Anderson's filmography. Except for *Bottle Rocket*, the director's first film, and *The Darjeeling Limited*, his darkest and arguably most despairing, every one of Anderson's works is presented in the context of some form of presentational device or framing narrative: the act breaks and theatrical curtains in *Rushmore*, the novelistic conceit and chapter titles in *The Royal Tenenbaums*, the filmic intertitles borrowed from the style of Zissou's own films in *The Life Aquatic*, the storybook opening of *Fantastic Mr. Fox*, the meteorological narrator in *Moonrise Kingdom*, and the nested framing stories of *The Grand Budapest Hotel*. Numerous observers have likened these techniques to tactics of Brechtian alienation, but Anderson himself denies that influence or that intention. "I don't so much connect to this sort of Brecht idea or response to being distanced," he has said, admitting "I don't know what tradition to refer to" in his penchant for framing and direct address (Seitz 282). Regardless of their potential alienating effects, the framing devices of Anderson's films make explicit the usually implicit desire that the work be *received* in some way—attended like a play, picked up like a book, listened to like a story, or, recursively, watched like a film. In the same way that Stewart says that the collection necessitates "the creation of an individual perceiving and apprehending" (154) it, Anderson's films—like so many of the characters within those films—plaintively ask to be acknowledged and regarded. They demand our attention. They wish to be transmitted.

If the collection is always a response to an aching perception of loss and an acute fear of dispersion, this too is part of that condition. Anderson's films always include at or near their center a character left alone in some way in the world or nearly so or in danger of being so. The fear these characters confront is the fear of isolation and estrangement, the fear of being made mute and alone, which also is to say the fear of annihilation without memorialization. Insofar as we make art to impose some kind of order on the world—be it in books or in films, in world-class fine art collections or in the arrangements of soldiers or airplanes in a child's room—we also do so to transmit and communicate that order to others, to create some marker of ourselves in the wider world. Anderson's films instantiate and record that process. At the end of *The Grand Budapest Hotel* stands a single image that speaks directly to this general phenomenon. We are back after all the twists and turns of the nested narratives at the towering stone funeral monument with which the film began, the gravesite of the beloved writer who wrote the novel from which the story of the film is supposedly taken. Covering that monument is an eclectic collection of keys affixed there by devotees of his work,

Figure 24. Regarding the author of the collection |

an emblem of their appreciation and an act of continual engagement. Regarding the monument is a young reader who has brought a copy of the writer's most famous book to his grave, enacting a transmission across the generations and receiving an inheritance as important as any family heirloom (fig. 24). On that funeral monument that has become the site of a collection in which all are invited to participate is written a single word: Author.

Notes

1. For the fullest application yet of Sconce's idea of the "smart film" to Anderson's work, see the chapter on Anderson in Perkins.

2. Benjamin is quoting in part from von Boehn, 136.

3. On the burgeoning subgenre of Wes Anderson parodies, see, for example, Houston or Stice.

4. See also Blume and Linden.

5. See, for example, Seitz's comment to Anderson on *The Life Aquatic* that "the seminal influence of *Star Wars* comes full circle here, because in this film, even more so than in *The Royal Tenenbaums*, you're creating an entire universe" (182).

6. See, for instance, Bordwell, "Wesworld," Foxley, and Rocchi.

7. "Proven Pointers for Visual Storytelling" (Barry Braverman interview with *Lights Film School*, Dec. 31, 2013). In one interview, Jeff Goldblum describes in particular detail the degree of Anderson's visual preparations for his films:

"He had . . . an animated version of the movie. It was a beautifully animated version of the whole movie, with all the cuts as they pretty much I think wound up to be. And he voiced all the characters. He called it animatics. I had it on my computer, you could see the whole movie" (qtd. in Jordan Zakarin. See also Seitz 299).

8. On this point, see Bordwell, "Wes Anderson," 240.

9. On these points, see Seitz 96–97 and 120.

10. Perhaps the only other major director to use the technique so regularly into the later twentieth century is Yasujirō Ozu, a connection Bordwell briefly explores.

11. See Ronson.

12. See Gilchrist.

13. When questions of the degree of letterboxing within these general aspect ratios are introduced, the already complex visual arrangement of *The Grand Budapest Hotel* grows even more labyrinthine. For the fullest account of these intricacies, see Bordwell, "Wes Anderson."

14. Regarding the jaguar shark, see Seitz 187.

15. On the connections between Anderson's films and children's literature in particular, see Kunze.

16. See, for instance, Tyree's inclusion of *Tenenbaums* in his description of "the movement of Anderson's camera through the rooms of the house in *The Royal Tenenbaums*, the ship in *The Life Aquatic with Steve Zissou*, and the train in *The Darjeeling Limited*" (Tyree 24).

17. Anderson's interracial couples include Anthony and Inez, reunited at the end of *Bottle Rocket*; Max Fischer and Margaret Yang, who unite at the end of *Rushmore*; Etheline and Henry, who marry at the end of *The Royal Tenenbaums*; and Zero and Agatha, who marry at the end of *The Grand Budapest Hotel*.

18. Probably the most comprehensive repository of cultural production by Anderson fans is the Tumblr account "Cuss Yeah Wes," whose mission statement is to "share the very best of writer and director Wes Anderson, by his fans, for his fans." See cussyeah-wesanderson.tumblr.com.

19. On the history of the DVD feature, see Stein.

The Reorganization of Life: |
An Interview with Wes Anderson

The following interview was conducted by Stéphane Delorme and Jean-Philippe Tesse on April 3, 2012, and published in issue No. 678 (May 2012) of the famed French film journal *Cahiers du Cinéma*. It is presented here for the first time in English in an original translation by the author.

Wes Anderson remembers he was somewhere in Illinois. A train that had departed from New York was taking him to California, and it was by telephone from his railcar that he had given us an interview about *Fantastic Mr. Fox* (which appeared in issue No. 653). This time we are in Paris and the paint is fresh in this beautiful apartment in the Sixth Arrondissement, still almost empty, where the U.S. filmmaker is preparing to install his new offices. For the first time, he has presented a film at Cannes, *Moonrise Kingdom*, which had the honor of opening the competition. Sporting a striking beige velvet suit, Wes Anderson puts his slender hands on the April issue of *Cahiers* we just brought him, stopping on the pages devoted to Martin Rosen's *Plague Dogs*, a film he loves, and on some documents provided by the script supervisor Sylvette Baudrot. Even if he asks about some translations ("How do you say blink in French?" [*cligner*] "And slow motion?" [*ralenti*]), this adopted Parisian always speaks in English.

CAHIERS DU CINÉMA: Did you write *Moonrise Kingdom* in the United States?

WES ANDERSON: I was often in Italy during writing, but I was in the United States throughout preproduction. I did the postproduction in New York—we installed the editing room in an apartment very close to mine. Every morning I walked over there, it was nice.

CC: *Moonrise Kingdom* is a very different film from your others, an outdoor film about first love, with children . . .

WA: People talk about similarities and differences, but for me every film is different. Although my approach is always the same, I still learn from film to film. In *Moonrise Kingdom*, the biggest novelty was the large number of outdoor scenes. I had already gone outdoors quite a bit for *The Life Aquatic*, but this was different. Here, the only way to prepare for certain sequences was to take long walks in the natural environment, take a lot of pictures, and study them. But that never really captures the feel of the place. A lot of the scenes were shot at first without the actors, with just me and a small team.

I wanted to know in advance, before the real shooting, what it was going to be like. It was very time-consuming. On the other hand, for the opening scene, I had no need to practice in advance because the sequence was very structured, the plans were all very well prepared.

CC: How did you find your two young actors?

WA: Ah, casting. Casting children is very difficult, it can take months. I started a year and a half before the shooting. And I watched lots of videos of children until that day when, as is always the case when you cast, we suddenly say: this is it. Kara Hayward, who plays Suzy, was wonderful in her audition. I saw thousands of girls play the same scene; it was boring, fake, I hated the scene, and suddenly, she appeared, and it was like she invented the dialogue. She had incredible spontaneity.

CC: This is the first time that your heroes have been children. How did you start writing? Were the adults added in afterward?

WA: The first inspiration was simply the story of two twelve-year-old kids who fall in love, but this feeling is too powerful for them, and they are overwhelmed. The film grew out of this, narrating a child's experience. But turning that idea into story doesn't just mean building scenes around a certain point of departure. Besides, I never write the scenes in order; instead I have ideas for scenes that I try to put here and there in the story, it's like a puzzle.

CC: Where does your obsession come from with those characters who, like your *mise-en-scène*, are hyperorganized? It is as if, for them, planning everything was the way to access the meaning of life, or at least achieve some kind of harmony.

WA: I don't know whether they find the meaning of life. We should probably assume that we will never discover it. The organization is a kind of metaphor for art: reorganizing life in such a way that everything makes sense. We are all looking for harmony, for inspiration. And sometimes when regarding a work of art, one has the feeling that this work explains us, touches our identity. For me, this is the strongest experience of art.

CC: Your visual design is always filled with details. Do you dream up all this while you're writing or when you're actually in the design, on the set?

WA: It depends. There are some things that I've added on set. But I put a lot of that information in the screenplay, simply because once we're on set, it's sometimes overlooked. If an idea comes to us on the set, we don't necessarily have what it takes on hand to achieve it. And since time is precious, we cannot always take the time to find or make what you need. Especially outdoors. In fact, what is really spontaneous on set concerns the actors. I know some people don't like my films because there are too many details that seem unnecessary. But there was a time in my career, early on, when I decided not to worry myself about that and just do what I wanted. I can't be thinking about what this or that viewer will think while I'm filming; I have to do what I love and stay focused on my story, the little world I'm trying to create. There are too many details only if I feel it is too much. It's totally subjective. But at least the film looks like what I want it to.

CC: Are there films that inspired you to tell this story?

WA: Yes, two English films, especially Ken Loach's *Blackjack* for the outdoor scenes, that feeling of being in the woods. This is a film from 1979 that depicts a love story between two children in eighteenth-century England. It's a bit of a fairy tale and at the same time there is something very realistic, very authentic about it. The other film is called *Melody* by Warris Hussein, a film from 1971. It also shows the runaway attempt of two children who want to marry. It's a beautiful film, the first screenplay by Alan Parker.

CC: *Moonrise Kingdom* is about first love. It's pretty rare in U.S. cinema to see this kind of story and the scenes that go with it: the first kiss on the beach, for example. Is this the heart of the film for you?

WA: It's the most important scene, the center of the film. Basically it's for this one scene that I wanted to make this whole film. The studio was very worried about the kiss because they were afraid that the film would be rated NC-17 [prohibited for those under 17, note]. It's crazy! That means *Moonrise Kingdom* would have been more subversive than Fincher's *Millennium* [French release title for *The Girl with the Dragon Tattoo*, trans. note], which is rated R! [restricted: for accompanied minors only, note]. In France I imagine that there would not have been any discussion about it. Obviously, I refused to cut that scene. Finally we got a PG-13 [not recommended for under 13, note], it's just two notches below the NC-17.

In this film, I tried to strike a balance between comedy and something more melancholy and to avoid giving more weight to one side or the other. And I wanted everything to be a bit abstract, such that the film wouldn't fall within any particular genre.

CC: That first kiss, it's the end of the journey. Like the jaguar shark in *The Life Aquatic*. Do you always have the end of the journey in mind when you start to write?

WA: Not necessarily the most important scene or the climax of the film, but at the beginning of writing I always have in mind scenes that do not necessarily appear to be crucial but that are important to me. For example, in *The Royal Tenenbaums* I had imagined the scene early on where Gwyneth Paltrow's character gets off the bus and walks toward her brother. It doesn't happen much, but it's the kind of image that you are working on unconsciously—you don't know why but you know the film will go through it, that it's a metaphor for the film as a whole. In

Moonrise Kingdom, the kissing scene gives the film its structure. There's a motion that leads up to that scene, and then everything stops when they are discovered by Bill Murray raising their tent like a lid. Then we start over again with the children's new escape, until the ending at the bell tower.

CC: There are beautiful uses of slow motion in your films, here in the wedding scene, for example. Why do you like this style so much?

WA: There is always a moment when I feel it is simply the best way to express a scene. On the other hand, I never think about accelerating the film. Who does that anyway? Kubrick's *Clockwork Orange*. . . . Do you know any others?

CC: Godard in *Band of Outsiders*. . . .

WA: Yes, when they cross the Louvre, right? There's also Agnès Varda in *Cléo from 5 to 7*, I think, in the scene with Godard and Anna Karina, but that's a film within a film. In any case, it's rare. It gives a comic impression.

CC: Slow motion can be very kitsch, but in your hands it gives a real majesty to certain scenes. The scene from *The Royal Tenenbaums* that you mentioned just now, when Gwyneth Paltrow get off the bus, is really magnified by the slow motion.

WA: Essentially, it shows that this scene mattered. Slow motion is wasted when it's not used properly. You have to have a very specific idea of what you're looking for, prepare for it well, don't improvise. There have to be counterexamples, documentaries with this kind of slow motion. . . . [He thinks] Oh yes, there are some in *The Thin Blue Line* by Errol Morris, but it's not very well known in France. Who are the best-known U.S. documentary filmmakers in France? Frederick Wiseman? He's also often in Paris. I ran into him in a restaurant recently. The Maysles brothers?

CC: Wiseman, the Maysles brothers, yes. In any case, you often use slow motion with characters who are walking.

WA: True, except in *Darjeeling Limited*: they run! I also like to show blinking in slow motion.

CC: There are often ridiculous and grandiose theatrical performances in your films, totally inappropriate for a school environment: the recreation of the Vietnam War on stage in *Rushmore* for example. Where does this taste come from?

WA: *Moonrise Kingdom* is a childhood memory—minus the scouts, since I was never a scout. But I really was in this show in school, Britten's *Noye's Fludde*, when I was about ten years old. I remember waiting outside before going on stage, in my costume. I felt the night fall and I heard the music inside. I'm quite fascinated by the theater, especially when the curtain falls and the actors bow, when they are still in costume but the expression on their faces has changed because they are no longer in character. I find it very moving. I also like the idea that the theater audience is perfectly willing to accept some very simple conventions. The principle of theatrical illusion, it's magic.

CC: Have you integrated other memories? The scene from the beach?

WA: No, unfortunately. This isn't a story that I experienced, but I remember I dreamed of living a story like this. So the film bears traces of my childhood imagination. When I was twelve, I wanted to live an adventure like this very powerfully. We read books of adventure in the hope that we'll experience one someday. This is related to the theater too.

CC: This is the second time, after *Fantastic Mr. Fox*, that you worked with the French musician Alexandre Desplat.

WA: The idea behind *Fantastic Mr. Fox* was that the music could be played by an orchestra of puppets. In *Moonrise Kingdom*, we wanted something more imposing, to give the impression of daydreaming children. So as they sink into the woods, the music swells and we up the percussion. They only cross a small island during the summer, but for them it's like an expedition in the Himalayas.

CC: The ending theme is wonderful.

WA: There are two parts. First Britten's variation on a theme by Purcell; we hear it at the beginning and I wanted to return to it at the end credits. Then, to complete the credits, I had the idea of a tribute to Alexandre Desplat. I wanted to do with his music what Britten did with that of Purcell, take each instrument and add them one by one. The little boy who announces it plays one of Suzy's little brothers in *Moonrise Kingdom*. His name is Jake Ryan. He's also the one who speaks in an advertisement that I did using stop motion for Sony. He came up with the text, a theory on how phones work using little robots. He has a lot of imagination.

Features

Bottle Rocket (1996)
USA
Production: Columbia Pictures Corporation, Gracie Films
Distribution: Sony Pictures Releasing
Producers: Barbara Boyle, James L. Brooks, Cynthia Hargrave, Polly Platt,
    Richard Sakai, Michael Taylor
Director: Wes Anderson
Script: Wes Anderson, Owen Wilson
Cinematography: Robert Yeoman
Editor: David Moritz
Original Score: Mark Mothersbaugh
Production Design: David Wasco
Art Direction: Jerry Fleming
Costume Design: Karen Patch
Principal Cast: Luke Wilson (Anthony Adams), Owen Wilson (Dignan), Robert
    Musgrave (Bob Mapplethorpe), Andrew Wilson (Future Man), Lumi Cavazos
    (Inez), James Caan (Mr. Henry)
Format: 35mm, color
91 min.

Rushmore (1998)
USA
Production: American Empirical Pictures, Touchstone Pictures
Distribution: Buena Vista Pictures
Producers: Wes Anderson, Barry Mendel, Paul Schiff, Owen Wilson
Director: Wes Anderson
Script: Wes Anderson, Owen Wilson
Cinematography: Robert Yeoman
Editor: David Moritz
Original Score: Mark Mothersbaugh

Production Design: David Wasco
Art Direction: Andrew Laws
Costume Design: Karen Patch
Principal Cast: Jason Schwartzman (Max Fischer), Bill Murray (Herman Blume),
    Olivia Williams (Rosemary Cross), Seymour Cassel (Bert Fischer), Brian Cox
    (Dr. Guggenheim), Mason Gamble (Dirk Calloway), Sara Tanka (Margaret
    Yang)
Format: 35mm, color
93 min.

The Royal Tenenbaums (2001)
USA
Production: Touchstone Pictures, American Empirical Pictures
Distribution: Buena Vista Pictures
Producers: Wes Anderson, Barry Mendel, Scott Rudin, Rudd Simmons, Owen
    Wilson
Director: Wes Anderson
Script: Wes Anderson, Owen Wilson
Cinematography: Robert Yeoman
Editor: Dylan Tichenor
Original Score: Mark Mothersbaugh
Production Design: David Wasco
Art Direction: Carl Sprague
Costume Design: Karen Patch
Principal Cast: Gene Hackman (Royal Tenenbaum), Anjelica Huston (Etheline
    Tenenbaum), Ben Stiller (Chas Tenenbaum), Gwyneth Paltrow (Margot Tenen-
    baum), Luke Wilson (Richie Tenenbaum), Owen Wilson (Eli Cash), Bill Murray
    (Raleigh St. Clair), Danny Glover (Henry Sherman), Alec Baldwin (Narrator)
Format: 35mm, color
110 min.

The Life Aquatic with Steve Zissou (2004)
USA
Production: Touchstone Pictures, American Empirical Pictures, Scott Rudin
    Productions
Distribution: Buena Vista Pictures
Producers: Wes Anderson, Barry Mendel, Scott Rudin, Rudd Simmons
Director: Wes Anderson
Script: Wes Anderson, Noah Baumbach
Cinematography: Robert Yeoman
Editor: David Moritz
Original Score: Mark Mothersbaugh
Production Design: Mark Friedberg

Art Direction: Stefano Maria Ortolani, Marco Trentini, Eugenio Ulissi
Costume Design: Milena Canonero
Principal Cast: Bill Murray (Steve Zissou), Owen Wilson (Ned Plimpton), Cate
  Blanchett (Jane Winslett-Richardson), Anjelica Huston (Eleanor Zissou),
  Willem Dafoe (Klaus Daimler), Jeff Goldblum (Alistair Hennessey), Michael
  Gambon (Oseary Drakoulias)
Format: 35mm, color
119 min.

The Darjeeling Limited (2007)
USA
Production: Fox Searchlight Pictures, Collage Cinemagraphique, American
  Empirical Pictures
Distribution: Twentieth Century Fox Film Corporation
Producers: Wes Anderson, Roman Coppola, Lydia Dean Pilcher, Steven Rales,
  Scott Rudin
Director: Wes Anderson
Script: Wes Anderson, Roman Coppola, Jason Schwartzman
Cinematography: Robert Yeoman
Editor: Andrew Weisblum
Production Design: Mark Friedberg
Art Direction: Aradhana Seth, Adam Stockhausen
Costume Design: Milena Canonero
Principal Cast: Owen Wilson (Francis), Adrien Brody (Peter), Jason Schwartz-
  man (Jack), Amara Karan (Rita), Wallace Wolodarsky (Brendan), Waris Ah-
  luwalia (Chief Steward), Anjelica Huston (Patricia)
Format: 35mm, color
91 min.

Fantastic Mr. Fox (2009)
USA
Production: Twentieth Century Fox Film Corporation, Indian Paintbrush, Re-
  gency Enterprises, American Empirical Pictures
Distribution: Twentieth Century Fox Film Corporation
Producers: Allison Abbate, Wes Anderson, Jeremy Dawson, Arnon Milchan,
  Steven Rales, Scott Rudin
Director: Wes Anderson
Script: Wes Anderson, Noah Baumbach (from the novel by Roald Dahl)
Cinematography: Tristan Oliver
Editors: Ralph Foster, Stephen Perkins
Original Score: Alexandre Desplat
Production Design: Nelson Lowry
Art Direction: Francesca Berlingieri Maxwell

Principal Cast: George Clooney (Mr. Fox), Meryl Streep (Mrs. Fox), Jason
 Schwartzman (Ash), Bill Murray (Badger), Wallace Wolodarsky (Kylie), Eric
 Chase Anderson (Kristofferson), Michael Gambon (Franklin Bean), Willem
 Dafoe (Rat), Owen Wilson (Coach Skip)
Format: 35mm, color
87 min.

Moonrise Kingdom (2012)
USA
Production: Indian Paintbrush, American Empirical Pictures
Distribution: Focus Features
Producers: Wes Anderson, Jeremy Dawson, Sam Hoffman, Steven Rales, Mar,
 Roybal, Scott Rudin
Director: Wes Anderson
Script: Wes Anderson, Roman Coppola
Cinematography: Robert Yeoman
Editor: Andrew Weisblum
Original Score: Alexandre Desplat
Production Design: Adam Stockhausen
Art Direction: Gerald Sullivan
Costume Design: Kasia Walicka-Maimone
Principal Cast: Bruce Willis (Captain Sharp), Edward Norton (Scoutmaster
 Ward), Bill Murray (Mr. Bishop), Frances McDormand (Mrs. Bishop), Tilda
 Swinton (Social Services), Jared Gilman (Sam), Kara Kayward (Suzy), Jason
 Schwartzman (Cousin Ben), Bob Balaban (Narrator)
Format: 16mm, color
94 min.

The Grand Budapest Hotel (2014)
USA
Production: Fox Searchlight Pictures, Indian Paintbrush, Studio Babelsberg,
 American Empirical Pictures
Distribution: Fox Searchlight Pictures
Producers: Wes Anderson, Molly Cooper, Jeremy Dawson, Christoph Fisser,
 Henning Molfenter, Steven Rales, Scott Rudin, Charlie Woebcken
Director: Wes Anderson
Script: Wes Anderson (from a story by Wes Anderson, Hugo Guinness)
Cinematography: Robert Yeoman
Editor: Barney Pilling
Original Score: Alexandre Desplat
Production Design: Adam Stockhausen
Art Direction: Stephan O. Gessler
Costume Design: Milena Canonero

Principal Cast: Ralph Fiennes (M. Gustave), F. Murray Abraham (Mr. Moustafa), Mathieu Amalric (Serge X.), Adrien Brody (Dmitri), Willem Dafoe (Jopling), Jeff Goldblum (Deputy Kovacs), Harvey Keitel (Ludwig), Jude Law (Young Writer), Bill Murray (M. Ivan), Edward Norton (Henckels), Saoirse Ronan (Agatha), Tilda Swinton (Madame D.), Tom Wilkinson (Author), Tony Revolori (Zero)
Format: 35mm, color
99 min.

Shorts

"Bottle Rocket" (1994)
USA
Producers: Kit Carson, Cynthia Hargrave
Director: Wes Anderson
Script: Wes Anderson, Owen Wilson
Cinematography: Bert Guthrie
Editors: Tom Aberg, Laura Cargile, Denise Ferrari Segell
Principal Cast: Owen Wilson (Dignan), Luke Wilson (Anthony), Robert Musgrave (Bob Hanson)
Format: 35mm, black and white
13 min.

"Hotel Chevalier" (2007)
USA
Production: Fox Searchlight Pictures
Distribution: Twentieth Century Fox Film Corporation
Producers: Patrice Haddad, Jerome Rucki, Nicolas Saada
Director: Wes Anderson
Script: Wes Anderson
Cinematography: Robert Yeoman
Editor: Vincent Marchand
Art Direction: Kris Moran
Principal Cast: Jason Schwartzman (Jack Whitman), Natalie Portman (Jack's Girlfriend), Waris Ahluwalia (Security), Michel Castejon (Waiter)
Format: 35mm, color
13 min.

"Castello Cavalcanti" (2013)
Production: American Empirical Pictures, Prada, The Directors Bureau
Distribution: Prada
Producers: Max Brun, Roman Coppola, Jeremy Dawson, Lisa Margulis, Julie Sawyer

Director: Wes Anderson
Script: Wes Anderson, Roman Coppola
Cinematography: Darius Khondji
Editor: Stephen Perkins
Production Design: Stefano Maria Ortolani
Costume Design: Milena Canonero
Principal Cast: Jason Schwartzman (Jed Cavalcanti), Giada Colagrande (Bartender)
Format: 35mm, color
8 min.

"Prada: Candy" (2013)
Production: The Directors Bureau
Distribution: Prada
Producers: Andrea Puig, Julie Sawyer
Directors: Wes Anderson, Roman Coppola
Cinematography: Darius Khondji
Editors: Dániel Hajnal, Benedek Kabán
Production Design: Stefano Maria Ortolani
Costume Design: Milena Canonero
Principal Cast: Léa Seydoux (Candy), Peter Gadiot (Gene), Rodolphe Pauly (Julius)
Format: Video, color
3 min.

"H&M: Come Together" (2016)
Production: H&M, Riff Raff Films, The Directors Bureau
Distribution: H&M
Producers: Matthew Fone, Gemma Humphries, Lisa Margulis, Julie Sawyer
Director: Wes Anderson
Cinematography: Bruno Delbonnel
Editor: Joe Guest
Principal Cast: Adrien Brody (Ralph), Garth Jennings (Fritz)
Format: Video, color
4 min.

Commercials

"Ikea: Kitchen" (2002)
Agency: Crispin Porter + Bogusky
Director: Wes Anderson
30 sec.

"Ikea: Living Room" (2002)
Agency: Crispin Porter + Bogusky
Director: Wes Anderson
30 sec.

"American Express: My Life, My Card" (2006)
Agency: Ogilvy and Mather
Director: Wes Anderson
Principal Cast: Wes Anderson, Jason Schwartzman, Waris Ahluwalia
2 min.

"AT&T: Actor" (2007)
Agency: BBDO
Director: Wes Anderson
30 sec.

"AT&T: Reporter" (2007)
Agency: BBDO
Director: Wes Anderson
30 sec.

"AT&T: Salesman" (2007)
Agency: BBDO
Director: Wes Anderson
30 sec.

"SoftBank" (2008)
Agency: Dentsu
Director: Wes Anderson
Principal Cast: Brad Pitt
30 sec.

"Stella Artois" (2010)
Agency: Mother
Directors: Wes Anderson, Roman Coppola
1 min.

"Sony Xperia: Made of Imagination" (2012)
Agency: McCann Worldgroup
Director: Wes Anderson
Principal Cast: Jake Ryan (Narrator)
1 min

"Hyundai Azera: Talk to My Car" (2012)
Agency: Innocean
Director: Wes Anderson
30 sec.

"Hyundai Azera: Modern Life" (2012)
Agency: Innocean
Director: Wes Anderson
30 sec.

Abbas, Ackbar. "Walter Benjamin's Collector: The Fate of Modern Experience." *New Literary History* 20.1 (1988): 217–37.

Anderson, Wes. Introduction. In *Rushmore*, by Wes Anderson and Owen Wilson, xiii–xvii. New York: Faber and Faber, 1999.

Baschiera, Stefano. "Nostalgically Man Dwells on This Earth: Objects and Domestic Space in 'The Royal Tenenbaums' and 'The Darjeeling Ltd.'" *New Review of Film and Television Studies* 10.1 (2012): 118–31.

Benjamin, Walter. *The Arcades Project*, translated by Rolf Tiedemann. Cambridge, MA: Harvard University Press, 1999.

———. *Illuminations*, translated by Harry Zohn, edited by Hannah Arendt. New York: Schocken Books, 1968.

———. "On the Mimetic Faculty." In *Selected Writings*, vol. 2, part 2, 1931–1934, 720–22.

———. *Selected Writings*. Vol. 2, part 2, *1931–1934*, translated by Rodney Livingstone, edited by Michael W. Jennings, Howard Eiland, and Gary Smith. Cambridge, MA: Harvard University Press, 1999.

———. "Unpacking My Library: A Talk about Book Collecting." In *Illuminations*, 59–68.

Blume, Lesley M. "What You Should Know about Wes Anderson," *Vanity Fair*, Apr. 2014.

Bordwell, David. *On the History of Film Style*. Cambridge, MA: Harvard University Press, 1997.

———. *The Way Hollywood Tells It: Story and Style in Modern Movies*. Berkeley: University of California Press, 2006.

———. "Wes Anderson Takes the 4:3 Challenge." In *The Wes Anderson Collection: The Grand Budapest Hotel* by Matt Zoller Seitz, 235–50. New York: Abrams, 2015.

———. "Wesworld." *Observations on Film Art*, Nov. 5, 2015. http://www.david bordwell.net/blog/2015/11/05/wesworld/.

Braverman, Barry, interview with Lights Film School. "Proven Pointers for Visual Storytelling," Dec. 31, 2013. https://www.lightsfilmschool.com/blog/cinematography-interview-barry-braverman.

Bravo, Tony. "How Wes Anderson Created the Aesthetic of a Generation." *KQED*, Mar. 13, 2014. https://ww2.kqed.org/pop/2014/03/13/how-wes-anderson -created-the-aesthetic-of-a-generation/.

Brooks, James L. Foreword. In *Rushmore*, by Wes Anderson and Owen Wilson, viii–xii. New York: Faber and Faber, 1999.

Brown, Bill. "Thing Theory." *Critical Inquiry* 28.1 (2001): 1–22.

Browning, Mark. *Wes Anderson: Why His Movies Matter*. Santa Barbara, CA: Praeger, 2011.

Buckmaster, Luke. "Sexualizing Children, Wes Anderson Style; or, Why *Moonrise Kingdom* Is Weird for the Wrong Reasons." *Cinetology*, Sept. 1, 2012. https://blogs.crikey.com.au/cinetology/2012/09/01/sexualising-children-wes -anderson-style-or-why-moonrise-kingdom-is-weird-for-the-wrong-reasons/.

Chabon, Michael. "Wes Anderson's Worlds." *New York Review of Books*, Jan. 31, 2013. http://www.nybooks.com/daily/2013/01/31/wes-anderson-worlds/.

Cheah, Pheng. "What Is a World? On World Literature as World-Making Activity." *Daedalus* 137.3 (2008): 26–38.

Chow, Rey. "Fateful Attachments: On Collecting, Fidelity, and Lao She." *Critical Inquiry* 28.1 (2001): 286–304.

Collins, Jim. "Genericity in the Nineties: Eclectic Irony and the New Sincerity." In *Film Theory Goes to the Movies*, edited by Jim Collins, Hilary Radner, and Ava Preacher Collins, 242–64. New York: Routledge, 1993.

Dean, Sam. "Production Designer Mark Friedberg Shares the Secrets of Making the Cinematic Worlds of Wes Anderson, Ang Lee and Todd Haynes." *Politico*, Mar. 27, 2012. http://www.politico.com/states/new-york/albany/story/2012/03/ production-designer-mark-friedberg-shares-the-secrets-of-making-the -cinematic-worlds-of-wes-anderson-ang-lee-and-todd-haynes-067223.

Dean-Ruzicka, Rachel. "Themes of Privilege and Whiteness in the Films of Wes Anderson." *Quarterly Review of Film and Video* 30.1 (2013): 25–40.

Deleuze, Gilles. *Cinema 1: The Movement-Image*, translated by Hugh Tomlinson and Barbara Habberjam. Minneapolis: University of Minnesota Press, 1986.

———. *Cinema 2: The Time-Image*, translated by Hugh Tomlinson and Robert Galeta. Minneapolis: University of Minnesota Press, 1989.

Desplechin, Arnaud. "Wes Anderson." *Interview*, Oct. 26, 2009. http://www .interviewmagazine.com/film/wes-anderson/.

Eiland, Howard. *Walter Benjamin: A Critical Life*. Cambridge, MA: Harvard University Press, 2014.

"Film Review: *Fantastic Mr. Fox*." *therein*, Therin, Apr. 4, 2012. https://therein therin.wordpress.com/2012/04/04/film-review-fantastic-mr-fox/.

Flatley, Jonathan. "Like: Collecting and Collectivity." *October* 132 (Spring 2010): 71–98.

Fox, Jesse David. "Wes Anderson Made a Fully Animated Version of *The Grand Budapest Hotel*." *Vulture*, Feb. 28, 2014. http://www.vulture.com/2014/02/ anderson-made-a-fully-animated-grand-budapest.html.

Foxley, David. "Welcome to Wes World." *Observer*, Sept. 25, 2007. http://observer.com/2007/09/welcome-to-wes-world/.

Frampton, Daniel. *Filmosophy*. New York: Wallflower, 2006.

Gilchrist, Todd. "'Moonrise Kingdom' Director Wes Anderson on 'Stealing' from Kubrick, Polanski." *Hollywood Reporter*, June 11, 2012. http://www.hollywoodreporter.com/news/moonrise-kingdom-wes-anderson-kubrick-polanski-335930.

Gooch, Joshua. "Making a Go of It: Paternity and Prohibition in the Films of Wes Anderson." *Cinema Journal* 47.1 (2007): 26–48.

———. "Objects/Desire/Oedipus: Wes Anderson as Late-Capitalist Auteur." In *The Films of Wes Anderson: Critical Essays on an Indiewood Icon*, edited by Peter C. Kunze, 181–98. New York: Palgrave Macmillan, 2014.

Gorfinkel, Elena. "The Future of Anachronism: Todd Haynes and the Magnificent Andersons." In *Cinephilia: Movies, Love, and Memory*, edited by Marijke de Valck and Malte Hagener, 153–68. Amsterdam, Netherlands: Amsterdam University Press, 2005.

Graham, Mark. "The Meditation Collection Space." *Visual Arts Research* 40.1 (2014): 49–53.

Haglund, David. "Did You See This? The First Trailer for Wes Anderson's Next Movie." *Slate*, Jan. 12, 2012. http://www.slate.com/blogs/browbeat/2012/01/12/wes_anderson_s_moonrise_kingdom_the_first_trailer.html.

Hancock, Brannon M. "A Community of Characters—The Narrative Self in the Films of Wes Anderson." *Journal of Religion and Film* 9.2 (2005). https://www.unomaha.edu/jrf/Vol9No2/HancockCommunity.htm.

Hayot, Eric. *On Literary Worlds*. Oxford, England: Oxford University Press, 2012.

Hinckley, David. "Dad-Blasted 'Bottle Rocket' Never Takes Off." *New York Daily News*. Feb. 21, 1996. http://www.nydailynews.com/archives/nydn-features/dad-blasted-bottle-rocket-takes-article-1.726441.

Hirschorn, Michael. "Quirked Around." *The Atlantic*, Sept. 2007, 142–47.

Hoffenberg, Peter H. *An Empire on Display: English, Indian, and Australian Exhibitions from the Crystal Palace to the Great War*. Berkeley: University of California Press, 2001.

Horowitz, Josh. "Wes Anderson and Jason Schwartzman on Journeying from 'Rushmore' to 'Darjeeling Limited.'" *MTV News*,. Oct. 3, 2007. http://www.mtv.com/news/1571111/wes-anderson-and-jason-schwartzman-on-journeying-from-rushmore-to-darjeeling-limited/.

Houston, Shannon M. "The 7 Best Wes Anderson Parody Videos." *Paste*, May 27, 2014. https://www.pastemagazine.com/articles/2014/05/the-best-wes-anderson-parody-videos.html.

"How Did All That Movie Talent Crash?" *The Independent* (UK), Sept. 2, 2010. http://www.independent.co.uk/arts-entertainment/films/features/how-did-all-that-movie-talent-crash-2068908.html.

Hubbert, Julie. "The Compilation Soundtrack from the 1960s to the Present." In *The Oxford Handbook of Film Music Studies*, edited by David Neumeyer, 291–318. Oxford, England: Oxford University Press, 2014.

Jenkins, Henry. *Convergence Culture: Where Old and New Media Collide*. New York: New York University Press, 2006.

Jones, Eileen. "Wes Anderson and the Old Regime." *Jacobin*, Mar. 18, 2014. https://www.jacobinmag.com/2014/03/wes-anderson-and-the-old-regime/.

Joseph, Rachel. "'Max Fischer Presents:' Wes Anderson and the Theatricality of Mourning." In *The Films of Wes Anderson: Critical Essays on an Indiewood Icon*, edited by Peter C. Kunze, 51–64. New York: Palgrave Macmillan, 2014.

Kane, Ashleigh. "Wes Anderson's Insane Attention to Detail." *Dazed*, June 23, 2015. http://www.dazeddigital.com/artsandculture/article/25151/1/wes-anderson-s-insane-attention-to-detail.

Karpel, Ari. "Moving Storyboards and Drumming: Wes Anderson Maps Out the Peculiar Genius of 'Moonrise Kingdom.'" *Fast Company*, July 3, 2012. https://www.fastcocreate.com/1681005/moving-storyboards-and-drumming-wes-anderson-maps-out-the-peculiar-genius-of-moonrise-kingdo.

Keil, Charlie. *Early American Cinema in Transition: Story, Style, and Filmmaking, 1907–1913*. Madison: University of Wisconsin Press, 2001.

Kennedy-Karpat, Colleen. "Bill Murray and Wes Anderson, or the Curmudgeon as Muse." *The Films of Wes Anderson: Critical Essays on an Indiewood Icon*, edited by Peter C. Kunze, 125–37. New York: Palgrave Macmillan, 2014.

Kertzer, Adrienne. "Fidelity, Felicity, and Playing Around in Wes Anderson's *Fantastic Mr. Fox*." *Children's Literature Association Quarterly* 36.1 (2011): 2–24.

Kunze, Peter C. "From the Mixed Up Films of Mr. Wesley W. Anderson: Children's Literature as Intertexts." In *The Films of Wes Anderson: Critical Essays on an Indiewood Icon*, edited by Peter C. Kunze, 91–107. New York: Palgrave Macmillan, 2014.

Lamont, Tom. "Wes Anderson: In a World of His Own." *Observer*, Feb. 23, 2014: 12.

Linden, Sherri. "Perspective: Look beyond the Façade in Wes Anderson's Films." *Los Angeles Times*, July 1, 2012. http://articles.latimes.com/2012/jul/01/entertainment/la-ca-wes-anderson-20120701.

Lorentzen, Christian. "Captain Neato: What Will the Hipsters Be Remembered For?" *n+1*, Apr. 23, 2010. https://nplusonemag.com/online-only/online-only/captain-neato/.

MacDowell, James. "Notes on Quirky." *Movie: A Journal of Film Criticism* 1 (2010): 2–16.

Murphy, Mekado. "You Can Look, but You Can't Check In: The Miniature Model behind 'The Grand Budapest Hotel.'" *New York Times*, Feb. 28, 2014. http://www.nytimes.com/2014/03/02/movies/the-miniature-model-behind-the-grand-budapest-hotel.html?_r=0.

O'Connor, Derek. "Ohh La La: Watching Wes Anderson." *Wes Anderson Film Series* notes. Irish Film Institute (June 2012). http://www.ifi.ie/whatson/season/ooh-la-la-watching-wes-anderson/.

Olsen, Mark. "If I Can Dream: The Everlasting Boyhoods of Wes Anderson." *Film Comment* 35.1 (Jan.–Feb. 1999): 12–17.

Orgeron, Devin. "La Camera-Crayola: Authorship Comes of Age in the Cinema of Wes Anderson." *Cinema Journal* 46.2 (2007): 40–65.

Perkins, Claire. *American Smart Cinema.* Edinburgh, Scotland: Edinburgh University Press, 2012.

Pollard, Alfred William, ed. "Noah's Flood." In *English Miracle Plays, Moralities, and Interludes: Specimens of the Pre-Elizabethan Drama,* 8–20. Oxford, England: Clarendon Press, 1890.

Roberts, Sheila. "Wes Anderson and Adam Stockhausen Talk *The Grand Budapest Hotel,* Collaborating on the Film, Creating a Lush Cinematic World, and Varying Aspect Ratios." *Collider,* Mar. 26, 2014. http://collider.com/wes-anderson-grand-budapest-hotel-interview/.

Rocchi, James. "Wes World: The Cut-to-Fit Universe of Wes Anderson." *Rolling Stone,* Mar. 11, 2014. http://www.rollingstone.com/movies/news/wes-world-the-cut-to-fit-universe-of-wes-anderson-20140311.

Romney, Jonathan. "Family Album." *Sight and Sound* 12.3 (2002): 12–15.

Ronson, Jon. "Citizen Kubrick." *Guardian,* Mar. 26, 2004. https://www.theguardian.com/film/2004/mar/27/features.weekend.

Salt, Barry. "D. W. Griffith Shapes Slapstick." In *Slapstick Comedy,* edited by Tom Paulus and Rob King, 37–48. New York: Routledge, 2010.

Sconce, Jeffrey. "Irony, Nihilism, and the New American Smart Film." *Screen* 43.4 (2002): 349–69.

Scorsese, Martin. "The Next Scorsese: Wes Anderson." *Esquire,* Mar. 2000: 225.

Seitz, Matt Zoller. *The Wes Anderson Collection.* New York: Abrams, 2013.

Smith, Kyle. "'Grand Budapest Hotel' Is a Triumph of the Twee." *New York Post,* Mar. 4, 2014. http://nypost.com/2014/03/04/grand-budapest-hotel-is-a-triumph-of-the-twee/.

Specter, Michael. Introduction. In *The Making of 'Fantastic Mr. Fox,'* by Wes Anderson with Michael Specter. New York: Rizzoli, 2009.

Stafford, Barbara Maria. *Good Looking: Essays on the Virtue of Images.* Cambridge, MA: MIT Press, 1997.

Stein, Bob. "Mao, King Kong, and the Future of the Book: Bob Stein in Conversation with Dan Visel." *Triple Canopy* 9 (July 23, 2010). https://www.canopycanopycanopy.com/contents/mao__king_kong__and_the_future_of_the_book.

Stephenson, Barry. "'Filled with Ritual': Wes Anderson's *The Darjeeling Limited.*" *Bright Lights Film Journal,* Oct. 31, 2011. http://brightlightsfilm.com/filled-with-ritual-wes-andersons-the-darjeeling-limited/.

Stern, Marlow. "Wes Anderson Takes Us inside 'The Grand Budapest Hotel,' His Most Exquisite Film." *Daily Beast*, Mar. 4, 2014. http://www.thedailybeast .com/articles/2014/03/04/wes-anderson-takes-us-inside-the-grand-budapest -hotel-his-most-exquisite-film.html.

Stewart, Susan. *On Longing: Narratives of the Miniature, the Gigantic, the Souvenir, the Collection*. Durham, NC: Duke University Press, 1984.

Stice, Joel. "The 10 Most Whimsical Wes Anderson Parodies on YouTube." *Uproxx*, May 1, 2014. http://uproxx.com/webculture/the-10-most-whimsical -wes-anderson-parodies-on-youtube/.

Tashiro, C. S. *Pretty Pictures: Production Design and the History of Film*. Austin: University of Texas Press, 1998.

Thomas, Deborah J. "Framing the 'Melancomic': Character, Aesthetics and Affect in Wes Anderson's *Rushmore*." *New Review of Film and Television Studies* 10.1 (2012): 97–117.

Thomas, Sophie. "'Things on Holiday': Collections, Museums, and the Poetics of Unruliness," *European Romantic Review* 20.2 (2009), 167–75.

Turan, Kenneth. "The Gang That Couldn't Shoot, or Think, Straight." *Los Angeles Times*, Feb. 21, 1996. http://articles.latimes.com/1996–02–21/entertainment/ ca-38140_1_bottle-rocket.

Tyree, J. M. "Unsafe Houses: *Moonrise Kingdom* and Wes Anderson's Conflicted Comedies of Escape." *Film Quarterly* 66.4 (2013): 23–27.

Vallois, Grace M. *First Steps in Collecting: Furniture, Glass, China*. New York: Medill McBride, 1950.

Vittrup, Christian. Foreword. In *This Is an Adventure! Das Universum des Wes Anderson*, edited by Christian Vittrup, 5–7. Kiel, Germany: Ludwig, 2010.

von Boehn, Max. *Die Mode in Neunzehnten Jahrhundert*, vol. 2. Munich, Germany: F. Bruckmann, 1907.

Washburn, Anne. Introduction. In *The Wes Anderson Collection: The Grand Budapest Hotel*, by Matt Zoller Seitz. 9–11. New York: Abrams, 2015.

Weiner, Jonah. "Unbearable Whiteness: That Queasy Feeling You Get When Watching a Wes Anderson Movie." *Slate*, Sept. 27, 2007. http://www.slate.com/ articles/arts/culturebox/2007/09/unbearable_whiteness.html.

"Wes Anderson: Hollywood's New King of Comedy." *Independent* (UK), Feb. 8, 2002. http://www.independent.co.uk/arts-entertainment/films/features/ wes-anderson-hollywoods-new-king-of-comedy-9166950.html.

Zakarin, Jordan. "Wes Anderson's 'Grand Budapest Hotel': Director Made Fully Animated Version before Shooting Film." *The Wrap*, Feb. 28, 2014. http://www .thewrap.com/wes-anderson-made-animated-version-grand-budapest-hotel/.

Donna Kornhaber is an associate professor of English
at the University of Texas at Austin. She is the author of
Charlie Chaplin, Director.

Books in the series Contemporary
Film Directors

The University of Illinois Press
is a founding member of the
Association of American University Presses.

University of Illinois Press
1325 South Oak Street
Champaign, IL 61820-6903
www.press.uillinois.edu